New Retail
Raul A. Barreneche

New Retail
Raul A. Barreneche

Introduction:

Shopping by Design

In his *Harvard Design School Guide to Shopping*, compiled as part of an ongoing research project with several of his students, Rem Koolhaas posits that retail is the single most influential force on the shape of the modern city. The *New Yorker* architecture critic Paul Goldberger noted in his critique of Koolhaas's trendsetting SoHo Prada store (below and following page) that Koolhaas's "screed" goes so far as to suggest that "shopping is arguably the last remaining form of public activity. Through a battery of increasingly predatory forms, shopping has infiltrated, colonized, and even replaced, almost every aspect of urban life." Sze Tsung Leong, one of the *Guide to Shopping*'s collaborating editors, notes that: "Not only is shopping melting into everything, but everything is melting into shopping."

For Koolhaas and his colleagues, retail spaces—even more than the office, the gym, the urban park, the theater, the airport, the train station, the stadium, and other places of public interaction—define the atmosphere of a city. And in many suburban contexts, the local shopping mall represents the only significant public space. There is no main street, no Central Park, no agora. The community comes together around shoe stores, jewelry kiosks, and food courts. In the world's livelier urban centers, however, retail stores constitute just one of a great number of settings for civic interaction.

Surely, however, retailers' newfound interest in commissioning major architects to design their stores has little to do with the academic studies of Koolhaas and his students. Rather, it is part of a growing awareness of good design's power to boost the prestige, marketability, and sales of products—whether clothes, teapots and toasters,

Prada Epicenter, Rem Koolhaas / OMA, New York, 2001
Koolhaas mixed commerce and culture with a performance stage that folds down from a curving wood ramp in the center of the store.

Prada Epicenter, Rem Koolhaas / OMA, New York, 2001
Stepped wooden platforms opposite the Prada SoHo stage do double-duty as bleacher seating and display areas for shoes.

or apartments. It is a trend that began when museums around the globe, inspired by the success of the Frank Gehry–designed Guggenheim Bilbao, began hiring famous architects to design expansions and new buildings. Once they noticed how an architectural landmark could propel an institution and revitalize a city (the "Bilbao effect"), trustees realized the increased marketability to donors and visitors of a building designed by a name-brand architect.

At the same time, mass-market retailers like Target and IKEA realized good design was one of their biggest assets. The global giant IKEA had always valued affordable design, while the American chain Target decided to boost its brand by hiring Michael Graves and Philippe Starck, known for their architecture and interiors, and fashion designers Todd Oldham and Cynthia Rowley to design housewares and clothing. Combined with trendy advertising campaigns, Target's design-intensive strategy was a success. Now the real estate industry is following the trend. Starck has a global chain of residences called Yoo under construction in major cities around the world. In New York, Richard Meier and Charles Gwathmey are the latest architectural luminaries to become central to the marketing strategies of the apartment towers they are designing.

It is no surprise, then, that the image-conscious fashion industry would appropriate the strategy. By nature, the business has always been about design—what's changed is architecture's role in reflecting and helping build the identity of a label. It makes sense from a business standpoint as well as from a cultural one. Unprecedented media coverage of architectural projects, especially the well-documented rebuilding of the World Trade Center site in New York, and a widespread obsession with design and home improvement television, reveal how popularized design has become. To tap into this new interest, retailers know they must work architecture into the mix.

Fashionable Collaborations

The collaborations springing up between fashion designers and architects often bring together two interesting artistic visions such as Frank Gehry and Issey Miyake joining forces to design the avant-garde Japanese designer's New York flagship (page 36) or the irreverent Miuccia Prada calling on Koolhaas to develop a series of Prada flagships across the world. It wasn't so long ago that stores were the province of specialized retail designers under the watch of an owner or in-house designer. Most stores were treated as stage sets purposely cut off from the outside world to focus shoppers' attentions on the merchandise. Architecture, at least the kind practiced by Gehry, Norman Foster, and Herzog & de Meuron, had no place in the building of a fashion boutique, much less that of a supermarket.

That's not to say the retail world was devoid of memorable contributions by architects. In the 1970s, the avant-garde architects James Wines and Allison Sky of SITE and Robert Venturi and Denise Scott Brown created unforgettable showrooms for the BEST Products Company that bordered on giant sculptural installations. SITE's iconoclastic designs included "indeterminate" walls and facades that looked ripped and pulled apart (opposite). Venturi and Scott Brown's BEST Catalog Showroom was wallpapered in supergraphic floral patterns (opposite), while its Basco store featured thirty-four-foot-tall (10-meter-tall) letters that spelled out the company's name logo in front of a boxy, windowless building (following pages). In the 1980s, Michael

Prada Epicenter, Rem Koolhaas / OMA, New York, 2001
A cylindrical glass elevator links the street-level entry with the basement-level women's department.

Prada Epicenter, Rem Koolhaas / OMA, New York, 2001
A wall with changing custom wallpaper designs, conceived of as an art installation, runs along the center of Prada SoHo.

Graves captured the style of the moment in a postmodern showroom for fashion icon Diane von Furstenberg. The store, in the base of New York's historic Sherry-Netherland Hotel on Fifth Avenue, was later taken over by and remodeled by Geoffrey Beene. In an era when stand-alone stores were less common than in-house boutiques in big department stores, these freestanding showpieces stood out from the retail landscape. Unfortunately, neither SITE nor Venturi, Scott Brown's creations stood the test of time, as neither exists today.

In those days, certain architects did not often deign to design fashion boutiques when they could make museums, skyscrapers, or university buildings. It is difficult to imagine I.M. Pei designing a store for Halston or Renzo Piano and Richard Rogers, fresh from unveiling the Pompidou Centre in Paris, creating a showroom for Valentino. The inverse was also true. The mainstream designers did not conceive of asking the architects behind the high-profile buildings of the day to give shape to their stores. (The SITE and Venturi–Scott Brown collaborations for BEST and Basco were anomalies. And while the projects were notable works of architecture in their day, the clients behind them were not the most well-known retailers, and the architects, though influential, were not yet renowned.) The recent pairing of big-name fashion houses and big-name architects reveals how much the cultural climate has changed.

One of the first designers to give momentum to hiring significant architects was Calvin Klein, who tapped the British architect John Pawson to shape his Madison Avenue flagship in the 1990s (following pages). Combining Pawson's minimal sensibility and Klein's pared-down,

modern tailoring was an ideal match. The ethereal store, which opened in 1996, was completely white from top to bottom. Pawson went against the age-old retail strategy of putting products front and center in eye-catching racks and display cases. Instead, he tucked clothes off to the sides and made displays as invisible as possible. What stood out was empty space, not merchandise. It was a radical proposition, but as with Klein's provocative strategies of the past—risqué ads for jeans in the 1980s starring Brooke Shields and a later campaign inspired by low-budget "kiddie porn"—it paid off. The Madison Avenue store was a hit with the fashion crowd.

The store started a trend toward striking, minimalist interiors that surrounded clothes with tantalizing emptiness— the architectural equivalent of white space on the printed page. The German designer Jil Sander hired New York architect Michael Gabellini to design her flagship stores in Paris, Milan, and London and her Hamburg headquarters, a luminous renovation of a nineteenth-century villa. Like Klein and Pawson, Sander and Gabellini shared sympathetic artistic sensibilities. The Hamburg-born Sander is known for sumptuous clothes with clean, minimalist lines and classic tailoring, and Gabellini's architecture possesses a similarly understated touch. The fruitful pairing resulted in more than eighty Jil Sander locations designed by Gabellini over a decade.

Meanwhile, the art world was also gravitating toward minimalist galleries, designed by architects such as Richard Gluckman, Frederick Fisher, and Annabelle Selldorf. The links between fashion and art deepened. Gluckman, an artworld favorite who gave shape to several of New York's top contemporary galleries made the leap to fashion. He

Indeterminate Facade Showroom, SITE, Houston, 1975
James Wines' design for a BEST Products Showroom
blurred the lines between architecture and landscape art.

BEST Catalog Showroom, VSBA, Langhorne, 1978
Robert Venturi and Denise Scott Brown dressed up
an otherwise banal box with their signature oversized
graphics in a design for a BEST Products Catalog
Showroom in Pennsylvania.

designed a Helmut Lang store in New York's SoHo and a parfumerie across the street that featured installations by artist Jenny Holzer. Gluckman went on to design another Helmut Lang location, in Tokyo, and, perhaps surprisingly, stores for the neo-baroque designer Gianni Versace in New York and Miami Beach, though none of these were built.

Global Trends, Local Style

Like Helmut Lang and Jil Sander, most successful fashion labels have stores around the world. These global operations raise the question of how stores in radically different contexts should be designed. If the merchandise sold in Milan is the same as it is in Tokyo, should the stores look the same? Would Japanese consumers want their branch of a Parisian couturier to be tailored to the Japanese market or do they insist on a bit of Avenue Montaigne in the middle of Ginza? Retail, in general, and fashion in particular, is an increasingly global operation, but the answer as to whether homogeneity or diversity is the better design strategy depends on the brand and the market. While some companies seek a standardized look to make all their branches easily recognizable as part of the same global brand, others tailor their store designs to the local market. Most companies settle for a mix of the two strategies, something between an off-the-shelf assembly-line output and an idiosyncratic one-off boutique.

The Dior store in Tokyo's Omotesando (opposite) combines elements of Dior's history and French style with a nod to the boutique's immediate surroundings, as well as the aesthetic sensibility of the label's current head designer, Hedi Slimane. The design is the work of several talents: The glowing glass exterior, reminiscent of layers of pleated translucent fabric, is the work of architects Kazuyo Sejima and Ruye Nishizawa of SANAA; most of the interiors are by Architecture & Associés and Dior's Paris-based in-house designers; and the Dior Homme area was conceived by Slimane himself. In general, the store combines high-tech Tokyo flash with soigné elements of Parisian classicism. In one telling moment that captures this cultural cross-pollination, pale gray walls with classical moldings that look ripped from a Parisian *hôtel particulier* surround mirrored display cases with the bright, flashy feeling of modern-day Tokyo. The rest of the interiors speak to Dior's fashion sense and Slimane's aesthetic inclinations: bold black acrylic and backlit translucent shelving and pivoting screen walls with video projections.

The stores designed by the modernist Isay Weinfeld in São Paulo (page 92) are a compelling mix of global fashion and design trends with Brazilian sensibilities of craft, materials, and lifestyle. Weinfeld's Forum store, commissioned by the fashion designer Tufi Duek, takes as its aesthetic mandate an interpretation of some of the inherently Brazilian themes that inspire Duek's clothing: the beaches of Rio de Janeiro, bossa nova, tropical fruit, and Cinema Novo. Neither Duek's clothes nor Weinfeld's interiors make a Carmen Miranda mockery of these ideas. On the contrary, Weinfeld's architecture is a neutral but rich backdrop to Duek's fashionable creations. The clothes do not play a secondary role, but Weinfeld keeps them off to the sides in display racks built into the walls, allowing empty white space to flow uninterrupted throughout the interior. Instead of clothing displays, seating areas with handwoven rag rugs from northern Brazil and classic midcentury modernist chairs by Brazilian designers dominate the sales areas. At the center of the store is a surprisingly tall atrium with a

Basco Showroom, VSBA, Philadelphia, 1976
Venturi and Scott Brown animated the 1,100-foot-long (335-meter-long) blank box of a Basco Showroom in Philadelphia with 34-foot-tall (10-meter-tall) letters spelling out the company's name.

Basco Showroom, VSBA, Philadelphia, 1976
Venturi and Scott Brown's Basco Showroom functions just as much if not more as a large-scale sculptural installation than a work of architecture.

Calvin Klein Flagship, John Pawson, New York, 1996
Pawson's striking white interiors and subtle displays made architectural minimalism in vogue for well-known fashion labels.

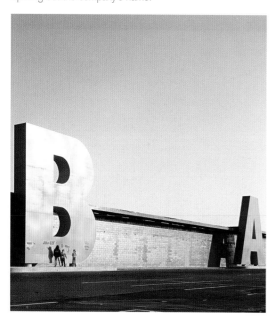

dramatic staircase covered in red glass tiles and a richly textured wall of *taipa*, the same indigenous material used to craft homes in the northeastern part of the country. Weinfeld's is a strikingly different kind of modernism compared with, say, John Pawson's utterly neutral, monastic style. Even if shoppers do not understand the architectural references to Brazilian building traditions, they can appreciate the breaks of color and texture that keep Duek's store from feeling like just another whitewashed shop interior. Forum makes for a globally fashionable and locally resonant shopping experience.

Weinfeld's design for Clube Chocolate, a "lifestyle boutique" just down the street from Forum, takes a more literal approach to bringing a bit of Rio de Janeiro to the crowded streets of São Paulo. The architect inserted an actual beach into a soaring skylit atrium that extends the full height of the store, with towering palm trees set into a sandy base at the lowest level. It's an obvious solution, to be sure, but it works. The beach is a central part of the cultural and day-to-day life of Rio, where Clube Chocolate originated. The palm trees and sand aren't empty signifiers of the Carioca lifestyle; the interior beach creates a focus for the café Weinfeld included on the ground floor of the shop and gives shoppers a break from the relentless urban congestion of São Paulo.

Clube Chocolate makes for an interesting comparison with Brazilian designer Carlos Miele's New York store, designed by the technologically minded architecture firm Asymptote (page 128). Asymptote partners Hani Rashid and Lise-Anne Couture went for whitewashed geometric abstraction of the things that inspire Miele, including the sensuous curves of the human body and the Brazilian landscape. The fact that the lustrous, curving display units that give the store its look were designed and fabricated with the computer relates to Miele's use of computer-aided cutting machines to create some of his complex clothing designs. However, this reference may be lost on shoppers who likely see it as another white-on-white boutique in a city full of such interiors. If revealing something of his Brazilian roots was really Miele's intent, then a design like Weinfeld's Forum would have made for a more legible abstraction of Brazilian influences. While Asymptote's subtle nod to Miele's influences creates an elegant background for his colorful creations, it falls short of providing instant brand-name recognition.

Prada's strategy of the "epicenter" goes against existing trends and sets a new standard for what makes recognizable flagships. Before Miuccia Prada and her husband and company CEO Patrizio Bertelli undertook the epicenter project, the look of Prada stores worldwide was defined by a single color: a minty green that covered the walls of shops from Milan to Miami, including boutiques within big department stores. There was no architecture to speak of in these stores, just painted surfaces in the peculiar shade that became recognizable to fashion insiders as "Prada green." In a sense, the strategy was an efficient one, with minimal investment in the build-out of stores but a high international recognition factor.

Prada and Bertelli's commissioning of Rem Koolhaas's Office for Metropolitan Architecture (OMA) to develop signature flagships in select cities was a radical departure from Prada's previous, almost nonexistent, architectural

Dior, SANAA (exterior) / Architecture & Associés with Hedi Slimane (interiors), Tokyo, 2004
Kazuyo Sejima and Ruye Nishizawa of SANAA designed the glass exterior of the Dior store in Tokyo's Omotesando to simulate layers of translucent fabric.

Dior, SANAA (exterior) / Architecture & Associés with Hedi Slimane (interiors), Tokyo, 2004
Dior's head designer, Hedi Slimane, created black acrylic and backlit translucent shelving in the Dior Homme section.

Dior, SANAA (exterior) / Architecture & Associés with Hedi Slimane (interiors), Tokyo, 2004
The store's interiors combine high-tech Tokyo flash with elements of Parisian classicism.

direction. The company decided that difference among the epicenters would be their defining characteristic; innovations in building materials, technology, and display techniques would be their stock-in-trade. OMA developed general ideas about the role of these flagships and designed three locations: one in New York, which opened in 2001 (pages 7–8); one in Beverly Hills, which was unveiled in 2004 (page 156); and one in San Francisco, which at the time of this writing is on hold. Herzog & de Meuron received the commission for the Tokyo epicenter (page 16).

Since the distinguishing point of the flagships was not architecture per se but, rather, innovation and experimentation, OMA and Herzog & de Meuron reconsidered every element of the shopping experience. Some of the experiments were simply formal variations on standard store elements. Koolhaas offered hanging cages of clothes, racks that could be rolled along on tracks like the movable shelves of libraries, and glass dressing-room doors that turned from transparent to opaque with the flip of a switch. Herzog & de Meuron created cast-fiberglass counters and fur-covered hanging racks. Other elements were more innovative, including the snorkel-shaped "sound showers" of the Tokyo store and a digital information system that let shoppers call up product information and images from a database while browsing through merchandise.

Commerce and Culture

One of the more provocative propositions of the first Prada epicenter, in New York, was not about materials or technology but about Koolhaas's introduction of cultural pro-gramming into a commercial setting. The concept is visible as soon as you enter the store: Koolhaas carved out a giant swath of prime real estate to create a curving, wavelike wooden grandstand and a foldout stage where intimate concerts and lectures could be held. The merchandise became secondary to this huge void in the center of the store. So far, the move remains more a grand subversive statement by Koolhaas than a functional venue, since regular cultural programming has yet to happen. "Meet me for a show at Prada" hasn't become a rallying cry of New York's stylish set. The retail spaces have been relegated to the back of the store and the basement. In that sense, Koolhaas's statement is a real jab at commerce, even though it is the raison d'être of his commission.

But Koolhaas's observations about the intermingling of commerce and culture have taken root in other projects. Federation Square, an eye-popping (and many claim stomach-turning) development in the center of Melbourne, Australia (below), is truly a mixed-use project. Offices, shops, restaurants, and an outdoor market commingle with a branch of the state museum of Victoria. Renzo Piano's Maison Hermés in Tokyo (page 166) includes a two-level gallery on its top floors where artists such as Hiroshi Sugimoto mount impeccable installations of their work. Herzog & de Meuron's Five Courtyards project (page 136), a shopping center in central Munich, deftly weaves together historic buildings and new architecture and contains a *Kunsthaus* among its clothing stores and cafés. Diener & Diener's Migros supermarket in Lucerne, Switzerland mixes commerce and education by combining a shopping center with an adult school run by the Migros chain in the same building. In fact, students on their way to

class can gaze down at the product-packed aisles that help support their education through corridors bound with walls of glass.

These projects reveal a synergistic relationship between shopping and other cultural activities. At the New York Prada store, Koolhaas attempted to overthrow commerce with culture; whereas these other projects take a complimentary stance which still supports Koolhaas's belief in shopping's cultural importance in the modern city.

Beyond Fashion

The involvement of well-known "starchitects" isn't limited to the upper echelons of fashion. Several years ago, the architect Carlos Zapata designed a striking outpost of the Florida supermarket chain Publix, in Miami Beach, with a sweeping metallic-and-glass facade (below). Zapata made shoppers part of the architecture by putting the automated ramps that transported them from the rooftop parking lot to the store, carts in hand, behind glass ribbons cut into the facade. Local residents took to referring to the eye-catching store as their "own little Guggenheim Bilbao." Dominique Perrault, an architect best known for the luminous glass boxes of the Bibliotèque nationale de France in Paris, also took a step back from such *grands projets* to design a series of supermarkets for the Austrian grocery chain MPreis (page 120). Zapata's mini-Guggenheim of a supermarket remains a one-off for Publix, but Perrault's designs are among several that MPreis commissioned from well-known and up-and-coming architects located in the Tirol region. The point of thinking outside the box and letting designers reimagine the standard supermarket as an eye-popping work of architecture is to add cachet

and value to the brand by adding a sense of style to its buildings. Given the choice between buying groceries in a windowless box or a sun-filled loft with floor-to-ceiling windows and a view of the Alps, shoppers would head straight for MPreis. Architecture is a draw and a boon to the company's bottom line.

The trend of hiring established architects to reshape overlooked retail environments extends beyond bland, big-box stores. The intention may be to create shops with the right look and level of sophistication for a product that itself embraces design. Such was the case when l.a. Eyeworks, a trendy, fashion-forward eyewear company, wanted an appropriately hip flagship store in Los Angeles for its line of glasses and sunglasses (page 114). They hired Neil Denari, an avant-garde architect and theorist who had recently headed the Southern California Institute of Architecture (SCI-Arc), to turn an old storage building on Beverly Boulevard into a cool composition of folded ceiling planes, angular display cases, and rollaway stainless-steel furniture. It's hard to surmise a default architectural style for a brand whose products are small bits of plastic, glass, and metal and whose ad campaigns feature the faces of pop iconoclasts like RuPaul and Boy George. Denari created an interior that doesn't have a direct correlation to the look of l.a. Eyeworks' products yet vaguely evokes the company's adventurous design sensibility and irreverent personality. Denari's design has muscle, with sweeping surfaces and unorthodox LED signs on its facade that make it clear there's a serious architect involved. For all its bold moves, however, l.a. Eyeworks' merchandise is still the main attraction. Long, mirrored display cases set into pale blue walls show off the eyeglasses in a flattering setting. Denari's architecture is not neutral, but it lets the glasses visually

Publix by the Bay, Wood + Zapata, Miami, 1999
The angular exterior of Carlos Zapata's design for a Publix supermarket in Miami Beach broke all conventions of supermarket design.

Publix by the Bay, Wood + Zapata, Miami, 1999
Zapata's design saved space on the ground by placing the parking area atop the supermarket structure.

Publix by the Bay, Wood + Zapata, Miami, 1999
Shoppers descend from the rooftop parking, carts in hand, along a motorized ramp behind the market's canted glass facade, making their movements part of the architecture.

pop against their surroundings. The project hits on one of retail design's biggest underlying challenges: striking a careful balance between the architecture and the goods. Ultimately, retail is about moving merchandise off the racks and into the hands of buyers.

The Swiss furniture company Vitra faced a conundrum when it decided to open a new retail store and showroom in New York City (page 142). For years, Vitra has been hiring stellar architects such as Gehry, Zaha Hadid, and Tadao Ando to design buildings at its main production facility in Weil am Rhein, Germany. For its New York location, the company tapped the up-and-coming Manhattan architect Lindy Roy. Her challenge was to come up with a design that would show off Vitra's new and classic furniture by the likes of Verner Panton and the Eameses in a suitably hip environment. Given their track record, Vitra was not afraid of commissioning sculptural buildings by star architects. But for the retail store, as opposed to a design museum or a corporate building, the furniture had to be given the starring role. Roy's design has just enough of its own character to make it memorable. The architect visually joined three levels of an old brick warehouse with a sculptural element that looks like a segment of a giant conveyor belt, stacked, of course, with some of Vitra's most famous chairs.

Designing an environment for a brand whose products are so imbued with a strong design aesthetic comes with inherent challenges. When the computer giant Apple rolled out a series of stand-alone stores around the world, it called on the American architect Peter Bohlin of Bohlin Cywinski Jackson (below). Bohlin, whose no-nonsense

modernist style is a far cry from Koolhaas's architecture wrapped in social criticism, may not seem the obvious choice for the innovators behind the iBook and the iPod. You might expect a high-tech architect in the vein of Greg Lynn or Asymptote, some purveyor of fashionable "blobitecture." Instead, Apple CEO Steve Jobs went for Bohlin's vocabulary of crisp, clean lines and neutral materials. Jobs wanted a design that could be easily rolled out in cities around the world and that resonated with Apple's aesthetic sensibility without replicating the look of any single product. Bohlin and his collaborators delivered variations on a standardized kit of parts—oversize Parsons tables in pale wood, cool stone floors, stainless-steel columns, and a structurally daring staircase of laminated glass—that translates easily between locations and captures the razor-sharp modern but not overly high-tech look of Apple's laptops, desktops, and peripherals. There's enough of a look to the stores' design to be able to recognize it as part of the brand, but the interiors let the products take center stage.

Choosing to evoke an overall spirit rather than a specific design aesthetic is often a smart corporate move. Apple's products are always changing and evolving. The shifts are slower than the seasonal cycles of fashion but still relatively quick. For instance, the curvaceous, jelly-colored computers popular just a few years ago now seem completely out-of-fashion, never mind technologically out-of-date. By getting to the core of Apple's aesthetic and distilling that visual philosophy into architecture, Bohlin ensured that the look of its stores would not be rendered obsolete with the next wave of sleek, smart computers. By all accounts, the stores are as big a hit as the company's

===
Apple Store, Bohlin Cywinski Jackson, New York, 2002
The Apple store in New York's SoHo translates the streamlined design sensibility of the computer giant's products into crisp, luminous architecture.

===
Apple Store, Bohlin Cywinski Jackson, New York, 2002
A large skylight at the center of the Apple flagship fills the interior with natural light.

===
Apple Store, Bohlin Cywinski Jackson, New York, 2002
A staircase with laminated glass treads echoes the sleek, technically minded design of Apple's products.

wildly popular iPods. They draw bigger crowds than the Gap. That's quite an achievement for a store that sells expensive digital equipment rather than ten-dollar T-shirts.

Shelf Life

Architecture for retail is a seemingly contradictory notion in terms of longevity. Buildings are meant to last for decades, while the exigencies of pushing products mean that the life span of a boutique or showroom may not be more than a few seasons. For architects working in this milieu, such short time lines are both a blessing and a curse. It takes Norman Foster far less time to see his striking boutiques for the British luxury purveyor Asprey in New York and London (page 44) come to life than his skyscrapers in Hong Kong or Frankfurt. But the stores, no matter how well crafted and conceived, will probably last for a far shorter time than his additions to skylines around the world.

Many architects base their retail designs on the likelihood of a short life span. Architecture Research Office's (ARO) design for Qiora, a cosmetics shop and spa on Madison Avenue in New York (below), incorporates luminous curved walls of translucent blue fabric in a dramatic yet inexpensive interior that is easily dismantled. At Mandarina Duck's Paris shop (page 184), Droog Design and NL Architects created a bold identity with funky displays—intended to be prototypes for other Mandarina Duck locations—that could be easily moved, changed, or taken out, leaving a blank canvas of an interior. It's a good thing, too: After twenty-eight months, the shop was dismantled and has since been bought and remodeled as a Helmut Lang store.

Whether a store lasts two years or two decades, it captures the architectural sensibilities of an era more plainly than maybe any other building type. Retail is about creating an environment reflective of the here and now: current trends, movements, aesthetic directions, whatever is in the air at a given moment. A store's design reflects the visual ideas of more than just the architect and client; it must be in sync with the look of a brand, the artistic vision of its designers, and the expectations of its customers. The projects featured in this book reveal that retail has become fertile ground for the world's top design talents. It is a market where, as in more and more areas of contemporary life, architecture matters.

=======================================

Architecture Research Office, Qiora, New York, 2000
The blue screens inside Qiora in Manhattan create a bold, quiet identity for the store through the glass facades.

=======================================

Architecture Research Office, Qiora, New York, 2000
Qiora's translucent screens were a simple, inexpensive way to divide interior space.

=======================================

Architecture Research Office, Qiora, New York, 2000
ARO's decision to use inexpensive, yet dramatic materials points to a consideration that is increasingly important when considering the short life span of many retail stores.

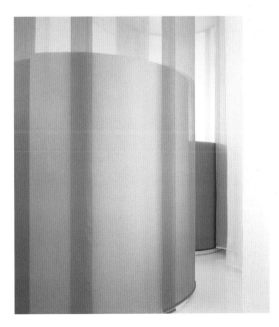

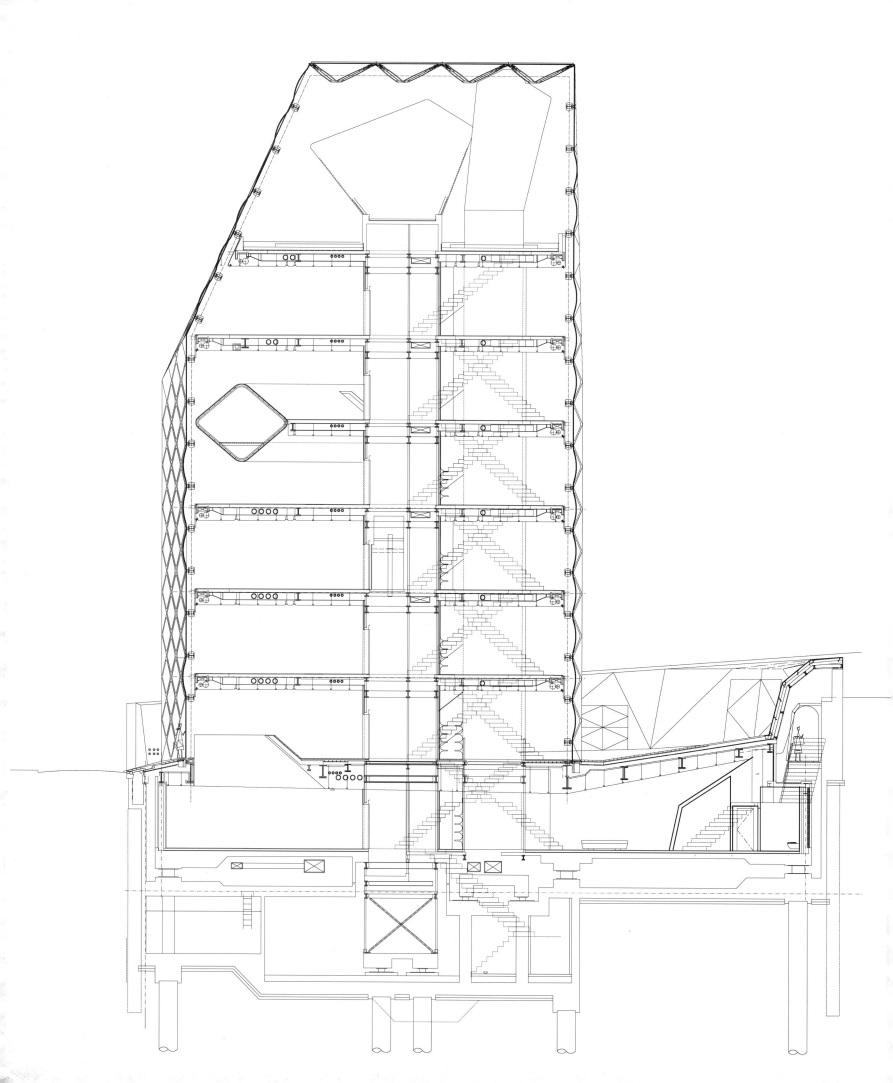

Prada Epicenter
Herzog & de Meuron
Tokyo, Japan
2003

BUILDING AREA: 30,785 ft² / 2,860 m²

The Milan-based fashion house Prada raised the bar for the architecture of its stores—not to mention those of other labels—when it opened a Rem Koolhaas designed flagship in New York's SoHo in 2001 (pages 7–8). The New York store was the first in a series of "epicenters" envisioned by Miuccia Prada and Patrizio Bertelli, Prada's husband and the company's CEO. Other outposts of this non-traditional flagship typology were planned for San Francisco (possibly can-celled), Los Angeles (recently opened, page 156), and Tokyo, the second epicenter to be unveiled. The Tokyo branch, however, was designed by different Pritzker Prize winning architects: Jacques Herzog and Pierre de Meuron. Herzog & de Meuron approached the Tokyo store, located in the trendy, upscale Aoyama district, not as a radical reconsideration of the shopping typology but as a rethinking of what an urban retail building could be.

The building's geometry defies easy description. The exterior form is reminiscent of a truncated rhomboid or irregular polygon, with five angled sides of different dimensions. As it rises, the building angles back to create a sharp, crystalline

profile that stands out from the crowded, low-rise streetscapes of Aoyama. The crystal analogy is reinforced by the store's luminous glass skin: 840 diamond-shaped panes set into an exposed structural cage of steel. Some of the rhomboid glass panels bubble out from the facade, creating a distorted optical illusion, and a handful of panes are curved inward, but most of the glazed skin is flat, making the building an almost perfectly clear box. Herzog & de Meuron say that such an exquisitely crafted building could only be the product of Swiss designers working in Japan.

The floor plans change in size and shape as the building angles upward and inward, but the four aboveground levels devoted to shopping occupy about three-thousand square feet (279

square meters) each. There is also a basement that is more than double the size of the other shopping levels and extends beneath a small outdoor plaza that adjoins the store. The outdoor space is an important part of Herzog & de Meuron's design as it lets the store sit back from the street and read more like an object than just another building. The inclusion of public space, a rarity in overcrowded Tokyo, also signals a certain sense of luxury. Framing the back and side of the plaza are canted walls covered in moss, a strange but extravagant touch.

The interior is as elegant and sophisticated as one would expect from an esteemed fashion house such as Prada. The carpeting and finely lacquered walls are a delicate white. There is so much visual energy created by the diamond-shaped

Opposite: Framed by a tiny urban park, Prada's new Tokyo "epicenter" stands out like a faceted gem in the crowded streets of Aoyama.
Above: The convex and concave curvatures of some of the diamond-shaped glass panels create optical distortions of the store's interiors.

Above: The upper floors open onto views of the Tokyo skyline.

Opposite: The main ground-floor entrance is a diamond-shaped glass portal opening onto a tiny plaza.

Following pages: The latticelike pattern of steel on the glass facades, evocative of oversize fishnet stockings, tweaks traditional ideas about store display windows (left). At night, the opaque tubes that traverse the glass volume are clearly visible through the gridded skin (right).

window patterns and Herzog & de Meuron's custom displays, which include cast-fiberglass counters and fur-covered racks, that the interior hardly qualifies as neutral, and certainly not minimalist. Views of the skyline, which act as visual wallpaper through the latticework of windows, give the interiors a serene quality in comparison to the glittering Tokyo streets.

Adding to the kinetic spaces are several solid tubes that skew through the interiors at unexpected angles and, on a structural level, stiffen the building laterally. Inside the tubes are cocoon-like dressing rooms and lounges equipped with one of Herzog & de Meuron's more innovative fixtures, the snorkel-like "sound showers" that play music arranged by the Parisian musician Fréderic Sanchez.

As Prada and Bertelli point out, Herzog & de Meuron chose to analyze the city and the ways in which shoppers would use the store and the products displayed rather than reinvent the entire act or typology of shopping. Their analytic approach has resulted in an exquisite, tantalizing building that engages the city, Prada's goods, and the consumer in a completely original way.

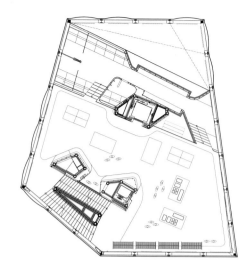

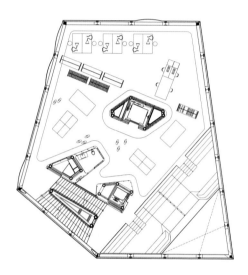

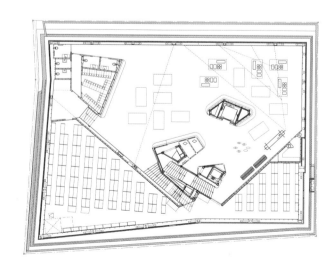

Above: Seen obliquely, the random pattern of convex windows creates a bubbling texture on the glass skin.

Right, top to bottom: Plans of the second, fifth, and basement floors.

Opposite: Herzog & de Meuron designed the store's displays, which play off the visual wallpaper of the city skyline seen through the grid of diamond-shaped windows, including exquisitely finished shelves and interactive video and sound monitors that the architects call "snorkels."

Following pages: The undersides of the dressing room and lounge tubes create a dynamic ceiling plane inside the store.

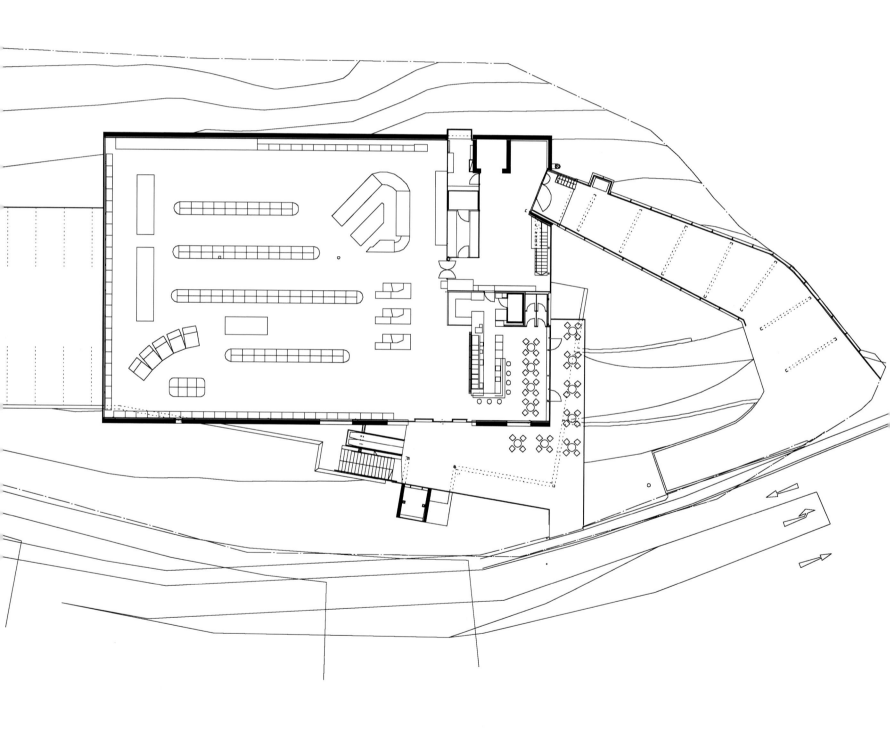

BUILDING AREA: 12,056 ft² / 1,120 m²

The modern-day supermarket is one of the standard-bearers of the derogatory label used to describe the huge, warehouse–like stores: big-box retail. The Austrian supermarket chain MPreis, which has 120 outposts in the picturesque Tirol region, is one company that thinks outside the box while functioning within its efficient confines. The corporation, a family concern that refashioned itself with the moniker "The Seriously Sexy Supermarket," has been commissioning up-and-coming architects to rethink its architectural identity. There is no design standard; architectural diversity is part of the company's strategy. MPreis's successful ventures with more than thirty architectural practices have made the company a bona fide design patron. It even represented Austria at the 2004 installment of the Venice Architecture Biennale.

The market designed by architects Rainer Köberl and Astrid Tschapeller in the small town of Wenns, west of Innsbruck, captures the company's vision of design as a central part of its brand image. The 6,455-square-foot (600-square-meter) building is still a box, but a crisp, well-detailed one. Instead of surrounding

itself with a sea of parking, Köberl and Tschapeller's single-story structure cantilevers efficiently over part of a parking deck to eliminate sprawl. The long ends of the box are built of white concrete with a random pattern of free-form windows punched out along the street elevation. A small café wraps one of the corners near the entrance. The short facades are floor-to-ceiling glass. In the daytime, the large glazed walls bring views of the lush alpine landscape and picturesque Tirolean churches and chalets into the store, making them a part of the shopping experience. At night, the store turns into a giant illuminated billboard—the actual signage, a backlit red cube with the MPreis name, is almost incidental to the overall image of the building as logo.

The interiors couldn't be simpler: The floors and solid walls are painted black, the ceiling is left as exposed metal decking with rows of fluorescent lights. The neutral, utterly minimalist palette has the effect of making the merchandise, not the architecture, stand out. Colorful produce sold in freestanding displays at the center of the store visually pops against the black floors and walls. Counter to the popular retail philosophy of shutting out the world outside to make shoppers concentrate on buying, the huge swath of landscape opened up by the glass walls doesn't intrude on the store. Indeed, like the store's attention to details, it proves that design adds value to the shopping experience. Why shop for food in a big bleak box when you can do it surrounded by good architecture and even better views?

Opposite: Set in a small Austrian town with picturesque alpine landscapes, the market's simple, boxy concrete structure cantilevers above a parking deck.
Above: A café wraps around the corner of the building below a large, backlit cube with the MPreis name.

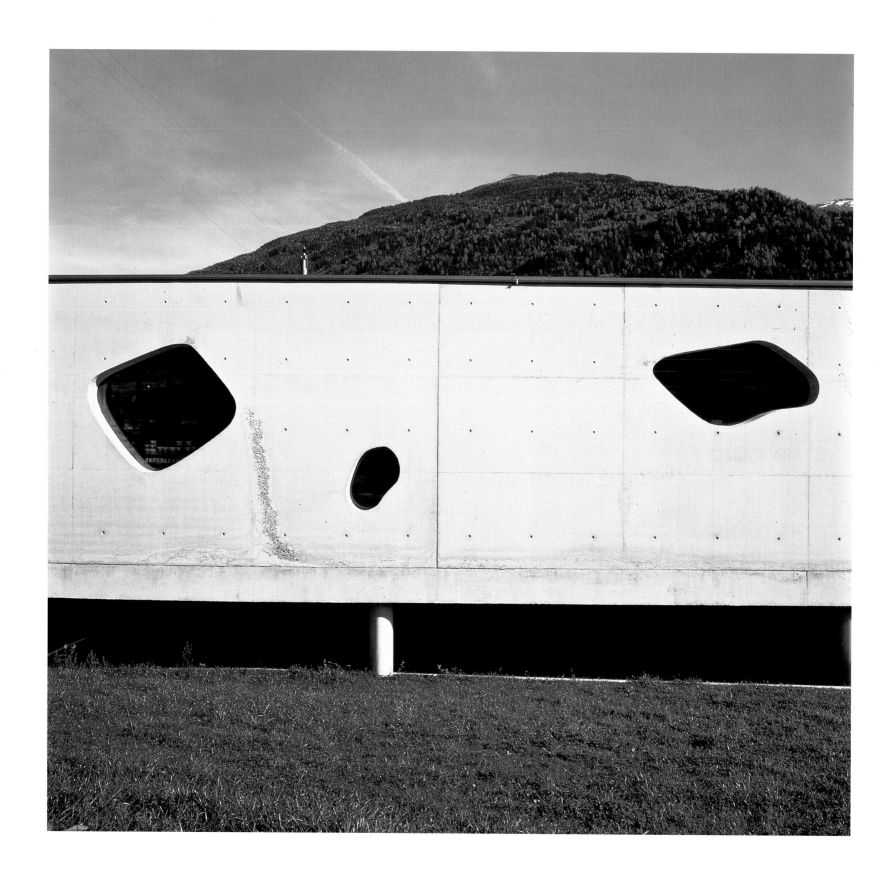

Opposite: The amorphous windows give the roadside facade's solid concrete skin a lighthearted touch.

Above: Free-form window openings bring light into a café area.

Following pages: Walls of glass make the alpine landscape part of the interior, but the focus is still on the naturally well-lit food displays.

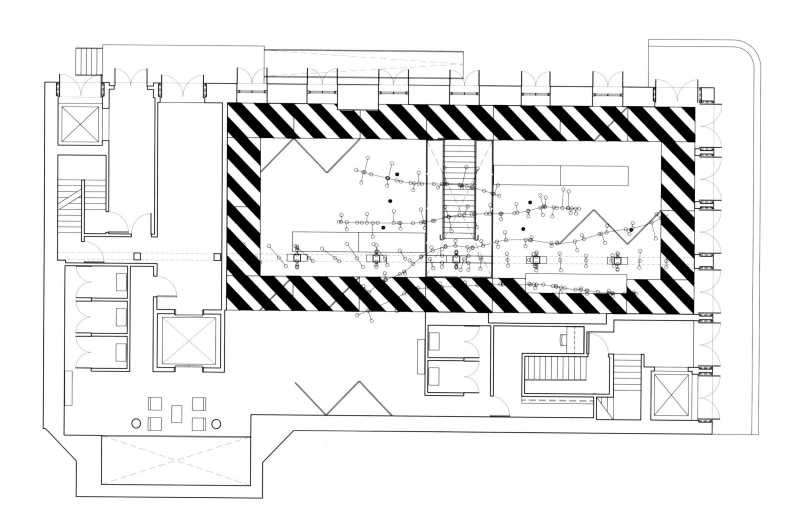

Issey Miyake Tribeca
G Tects / Frank O. Gehry
and Associates
New York, USA
2003

BUILDING AREA: 14,664 ft² / 1,362 m²

Gordon Kipping, a young New York–based architect who had taught a design studio with Frank Gehry at Yale University, collaborated with Gehry on one of his first big commissions: innovative Japanese fashion designer Issey Miyake's US retail hub. Miyake, a longtime fan of Gehry's, asked the architect to design the space, housed in an old cast-iron building in New York's trendy TriBeCa. Gehry passed on taking the commission outright but suggested Kipping's firm, G Tects, for the job of giving form to the narrative he and Miyake developed for the space. The two conjured up a vision of a tornado that sweeps the store clean, leaving in its wake a fanciful sculpture of titanium sheets whirling throughout the store.

Gehry art-directed the store's overall approach, while Kipping determined how to give form to Gehry's concept and handled the pragmatic aspects of design, such as restoring the 1880s cast-iron factory, securing approval of the local landmarks commission, and developing the construction details that would allow Gehry's tornado to take flight. Kipping divided the 14,664-square-foot (1,362-square-meter)

program into three levels: the main retail space on the ground floor; a showroom, a lounge for VIP shoppers, dressing rooms, and offices in the basement; and storage in the subbasement. Some daylight subtly works its way down to the basement level through glass pads set into the sidewalk outside and a swath around the perimeter of the sales floor that Kipping removed and replaced with slabs of glass. The dramatic slicing, visible as soon as one steps through the front door, reveals the wooden floor joists in a manner reminiscent of the artist Gordon Matta-Clark's architectural cuttings.

Aside from the gashes cut into the wood floor, the ground-floor space has a rough, industrial quality reminiscent of Gehry's earliest work, including his own Santa Monica bungalow. Exposed

ceiling joists and white walls make a neutral backdrop for the main attraction, the whirling titanium tornado. Kipping developed low-tech methods to construct the fluid metal sculpture. As with Gehry's bigger, better-known projects, including the Guggenheim Bilbao, the architect digitized physical study models on computers to make sure the built piece would match the billows and curves of Gehry's early maquettes. But here the thin titanium panels, the same kind used to clad the Guggenheim's exterior, attach to the interior structure with rubber-footed steel tubes, Velcro, and double-sided tape. The metallic vortex rises up from the basement, wrapping the walls of the staircase and columns on either side of the cashier, and erupts in a billow of metal ribbons reaching toward the front door.

Opposite: The titanium sheets are visible from the street through large panes of glass behind the historic cast-iron facade.

Above left: Kipping exposed the original ceiling joists and a section of the floor joists, which he covered in striped glass. The anime-inspired mural is by Gehry's son Alejandro.

Above right: Miyake's edgy A-POC clothing line (an acronym for A Piece of Cloth) is cut from a single roll of fabric, which Kipping displayed between a swirling titanium "tornado" suspended from the exposed ceiling structure.

Above: On the basement level, glass walls enclose a showroom that also functions as a retail space.
Opposite: Rolling display racks were inspired by garment-industry standards. Simple fluorescent strips are mounted to the exposed wood ceiling joists.
Following pages: Gehry and Kipping conceived a sculptural "tornado" composed of thin sheets of twisted titanium at the center of the store, beginning at the staircase leading down to the basement level showroom and offices (left). The metallic sculpture wraps the cashier (right).

In the basement, glass walls and sliding glass doors enclose the showroom, which doubles as additional retail space when commercial buyers are not placing orders on the premises. The space floats like a glass box beneath exposed wood ceiling joists hung with off-the-shelf fluorescent strips. Inside the box, custom-designed rolling display racks take inspiration from the industrial workhorses that are a common sight on the streets of New York's Garment District.

Miyake says he could not imagine an architect other than Gehry designing the interior of his store. A fashion designer with a strong aesthetic working with an architect with an equally distinct visual language could be difficult going in terms of both negotiating the creative process as well as creating a space that complements rather than competes with the clothes. In this case, the synergy between the two creative minds, aided by Kipping, seems to have resolved itself seamlessly.

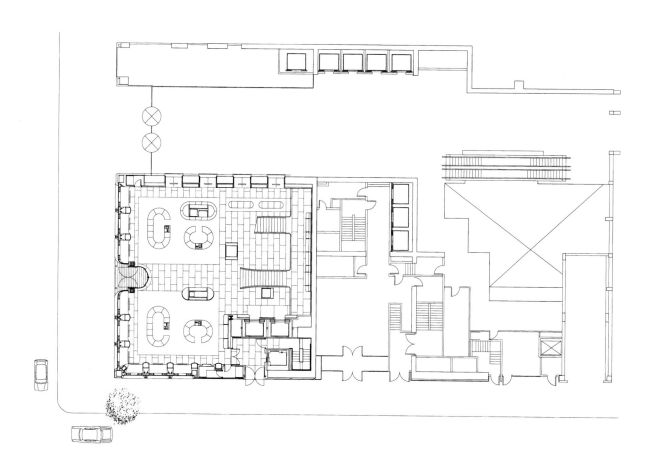

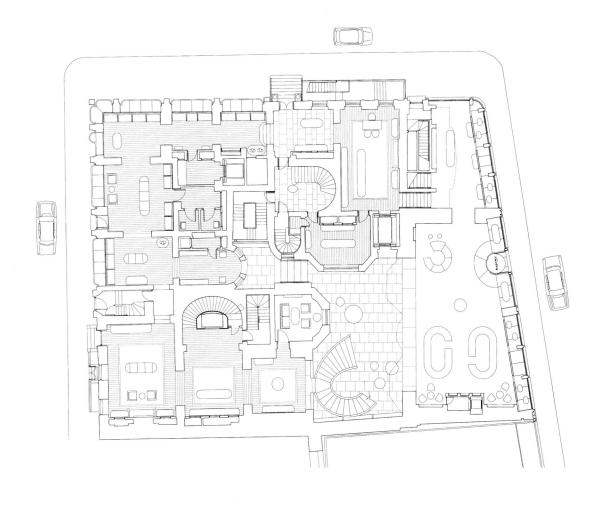

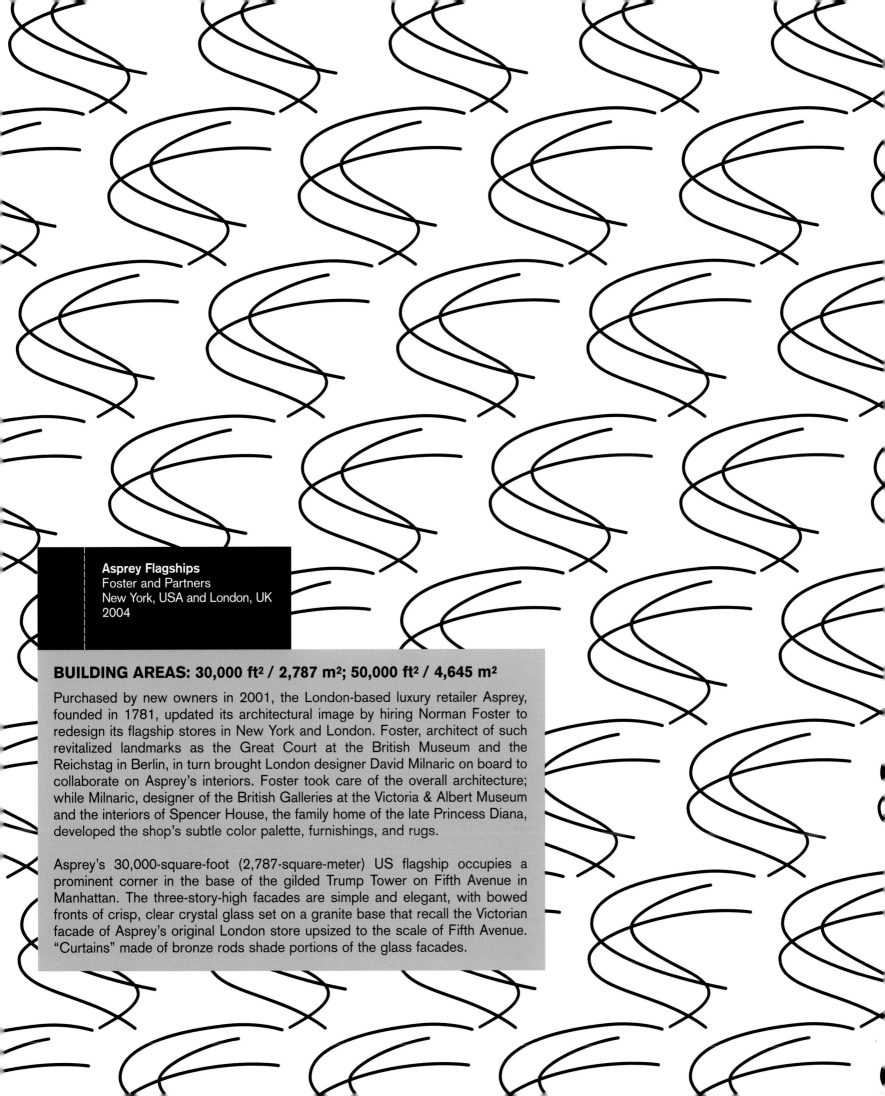

Asprey Flagships
Foster and Partners
New York, USA and London, UK
2004

BUILDING AREAS: 30,000 ft² / 2,787 m²; 50,000 ft² / 4,645 m²

Purchased by new owners in 2001, the London-based luxury retailer Asprey, founded in 1781, updated its architectural image by hiring Norman Foster to redesign its flagship stores in New York and London. Foster, architect of such revitalized landmarks as the Great Court at the British Museum and the Reichstag in Berlin, in turn brought London designer David Milnaric on board to collaborate on Asprey's interiors. Foster took care of the overall architecture; while Milnaric, designer of the British Galleries at the Victoria & Albert Museum and the interiors of Spencer House, the family home of the late Princess Diana, developed the shop's subtle color palette, furnishings, and rugs.

Asprey's 30,000-square-foot (2,787-square-meter) US flagship occupies a prominent corner in the base of the gilded Trump Tower on Fifth Avenue in Manhattan. The three-story-high facades are simple and elegant, with bowed fronts of crisp, clear crystal glass set on a granite base that recall the Victorian facade of Asprey's original London store upsized to the scale of Fifth Avenue. "Curtains" made of bronze rods shade portions of the glass facades.

Asprey's signature color is deep purple, but the interior of the New York store is sparkling white. Floors of British limestone and pale carpets set off Foster's custom freestanding and built-in display cases made of mahogany, bronze, and glass; sweeping staircases wrapped in glass balustrades with brass handrails keep the focus on the products. Like many elements in the store, the staircases and vitrines put a decidedly modern, pared-down spin on Asprey's most traditional elements. In one rare moment of brazen traditionalism, a mezzanine level displays Asprey's collection of rare books in a clubby space with period furniture and carpets selected by Milnaric.

Foster and Milnaric again joined forces to put a high-tech-meets-traditional-luxury spin on Asprey's London flagship and

headquarters. Since setting up shop behind a cast-iron facade on New Bond Street in the 19th century, the company had expanded into a total of five separate historic buildings housing the store, offices, and workshops for leather and silver. Foster's biggest challenge was weaving the disparate buildings into a functional whole. He cleared out existing roof structures, cleaned and restored the buildings' Georgian brick facades, and covered the whole ensemble with a delicate steel-and-glass roof in the same vein as his reworking of the Great Court at the British Museum. A sweeping spiral stair and bridges with glass balustrades link the different buildings and floor levels.

Along the main New Bond Street frontage, Foster removed an existing mezzanine to raise the scale of the main retail space to

Opposite: The facade of curved bays of crystal-clear glass set onto a granite base offers a modernist interpretation of the Victorian shop front of the original Asprey store in London. Above: The three-story Asprey flagship in New York occupies a corner of the base of the gilded Trump Tower on Fifth Avenue.

Above: At night, the triple-height exterior reads as a series of softly lit, delicately curved white fins behind the glass facades.

Opposite, left: Glass balustrades edged with brass railings give a transparent, clean-lined look to the glowing minimalist interior.

Opposite, top right: Screens of brass rods act like gauzy curtains to shade portions of the glass facades.

Opposite, bottom right: Glass-edged stairs wind through an atrium at the center of the shop.

a grander height. Throughout the interiors, the palette is subtle but rich: Venetian plaster, pale carpets, stone, leather, and hardwood. While the New York flagship is about clarity and minimalism, the architecture of the London store is more complex and varied. Enticing glimpses of other spaces pervade each room, whether the restored brick facades of adjoining buildings, detailed with Palladian windows and flower boxes, or the sculptural glass curves of the spiral staircase. The merging of history and modernity is everywhere, a perfect analogy to Asprey's new aesthetic direction and its honored roots.

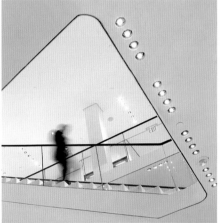

Above: Foster was challenged to maintain the
historic quality of Asprey's London flagship,
first established in the nineteenth century.
Opposite: A gridded steel-and-glass roof joins
the five different structures.
Following Pages: Restored Georgian brick exteriors
are now interior facades of the newly covered
courtyard (left). The interiors feature a subtle
palette of Venetian plaster, hardwood floors, and
custom display cases edged in bronze (right).

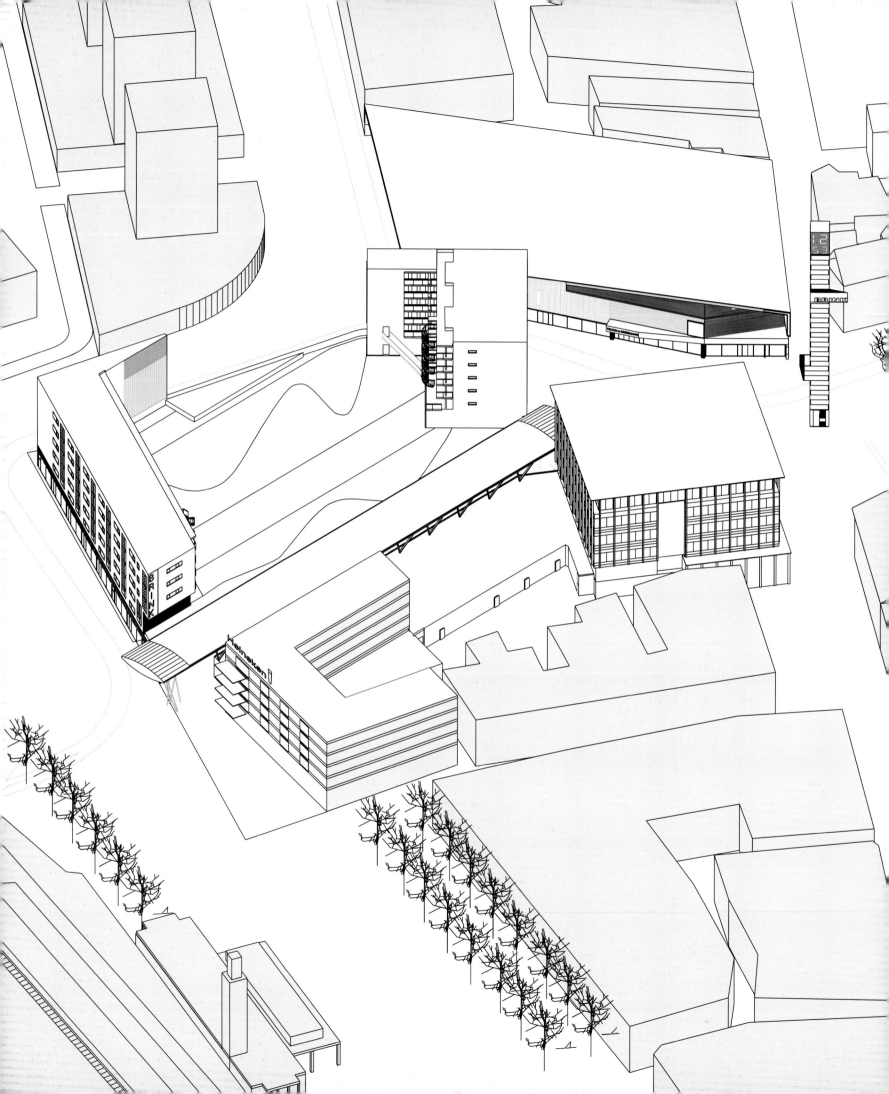

BUILDING AREA: 376,700 ft² / 35,000 m²

Munich architects Peter Wilson and Julia Bolles-Wilson designed a new *brink*, or village square, as part of a master plan to bring a pedestrian-friendly mix of housing, offices, shops, and transportation to the center of Hengelo. The Dutch town, located near the German border, suffered from both bombing during World War II and insensitive post war reconstruction projects. The site, where a demolished factory stood at the center of town, adjoins an existing outdoor marketplace and the city's main railway station. The architects removed a parking plaza and submerged a three-story car park beneath the new De Brink complex. The main retail components are a three-story branch of the Dutch department store chain Vroom & Dreesmann and a shopping arcade, sheltered by a canopy supported on canted columns, that links the rail station with blocks of apartments.

Vroom & Dreesmann plays a prominent role in Bolles + Wilson's urban ensemble, with a striking triangulated profile clad in the architect's signature palette of bold, dark colors. A large segment of the metal roof overhangs one end of the

De Brink Center
Bolles + Wilson
Hengelo, Netherlands
1999

Above: A new clock tower marks one edge of the new mixed-use complex and creates a counterpart to the town's historic church tower, visible in the distance.
Opposite: A shopping arcade, sheltered by a canopy supported on canted columns, links Hengelo's rail station with blocks of apartments.

tapered structure, anchoring the corner and mitigating the scale of the mixed-use complex.

Just beyond the department store is the most visible addition to the Hengelo skyline: a 144-foot-tall (44-meter-tall) bell tower clad in square panels of precast concrete. Atop the tower is a large digital clock announcing the time in towering LCD numbers; farther down the shaft, electronic billboards wrap the concrete base. The clock tower creates a new urban marker for the city as well as for the De Brink complex. Bolles + Wilson drew inspiration from the tower of the Lambertuskirche just beyond the plaza but made sure to make their stark, modern clock tower respectful of the historic landmark. The tower also acts as a linchpin between the historic market-

place, which is framed on three sides by existing low-rise commercial buildings, and the striking new structures of the Bolles + Wilson plan.

The original marketplace is an important part of the new De Brink precinct: Twice a week covered stalls fill the plaza as it transforms into a lively food and flea market. Other times during the year, the vast plaza is filled with fans listening to live concerts or children enjoying carnival rides. Throughout Europe, traditional arcades and open-air urban markets are still a vibrant part of daily life, even as American-style shopping malls encroach on these cities. In Hengelo, Bolles + Wilson struck a harmonious balance between the traditional market and the contemporary office and apartment block.

Left: Seen from the town square, the three-story department store capped with an angular roof cantilever anchors one corner of the mixed-use De Brink Center.

BUILDING AREA: 25,000 m² / 269,000 ft²

The visionary London architects Jan Kaplicky and Amanda Levete of Future Systems are known for free-form, fluid structures that seem to defy the laws of gravity. Their design for the Birmingham outpost of the London department store Selfridges also defies easy comprehension. Selfridges asked Future Systems to create a building that would need no sign on the door and that would attract shoppers from a twenty-five-mile radius around Birmingham. The unique and spirited design certainly accomplished that goal. The department store anchors the Bullring, a larger retail development intended to bring the moribund city center back to life. However, the rest of the Bullring complex has the overall appearance of an off-the-shelf shopping mall that seems even more banal compared with Selfridges' unexpected design.

The building's footprint covers 54,000 square feet (5,019 square meters) on a corner site between Birmingham's main rail station and historic Saint Martin's Church. The curvaceous form of the building is largely in response to the amorphous perimeter of the site, which dictated Future Systems overall design

Selfridges
Future Systems
Birmingham, UK
2003

approach. Future Systems then covered the five-story-tall exterior in sprayed-on concrete painted a bright Yves Klein blue and attached fifteen thousand aluminum disks to the underlying concrete surface. The effect is mesmerizing, especially when seen next to other landmarks of Birmingham's skyline. Future Systems also included outdoor balconies and glass-enclosed walkways that connect the massive store more intimately with the rest of the city.

Inside, the store is organized around two sculptural skylit atria framed by slick, white lacquered balustrades. The atria allow shafts of natural light to penetrate deep into the space. Elevators crisscrossing the atria appear to tie the large voids together; their smooth, white undersides giving them a strong visual presence. Future Systems designed only these open spaces and the ground-floor retail area, which houses a large food hall and design and children's-clothing departments. Acting as a type of master planner, the firm oversaw other architects for the rest of the floors. Eldridge Smerin designed the second level, which contains areas for books and electronics. Stanton Williams designed the third floor, with cosmetics, accessories, and menswear. And finally, Cibic & Partners and Lees Associates created the top-floor women's-wear department and the sleek Gallery restaurant. The towering skylit atria hold together the disparate look of the various concessions and departments and create a neutral backdrop for an interior that is as lively as the store's exterior.

Opposite: Ovoid glass cutouts in the metallic skin lead to outdoor balconies overlooking the city.
Above: The store's concrete exterior is covered in a grid of more than fifteen thousand aluminum disks.

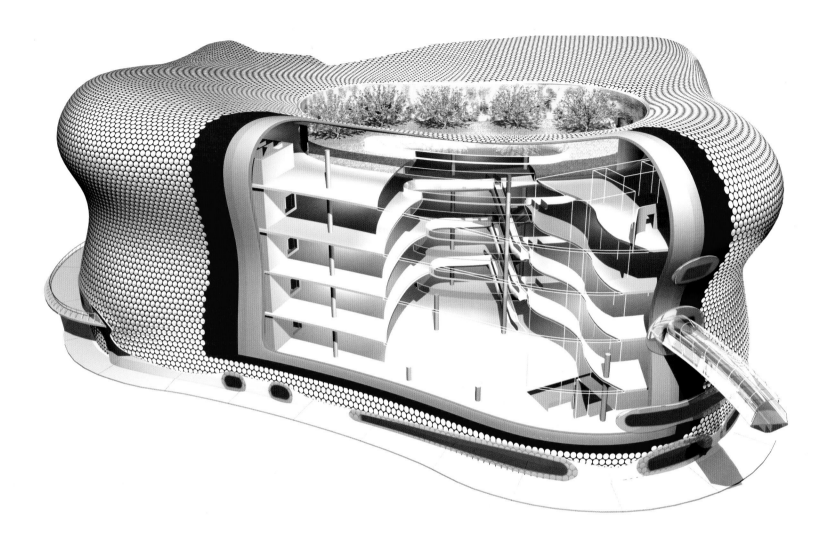

Opposite: A sinuous glass-enclosed walkway leads to a more conventional-looking parking structure across the street.
Above: Cutaway axonometric.

Above left: At night, the metallic disks take
on a luminous and reflective quality.
Above right: The bulbous metal-clad blob
winds its way mysteriously through the center
of Birmingham.

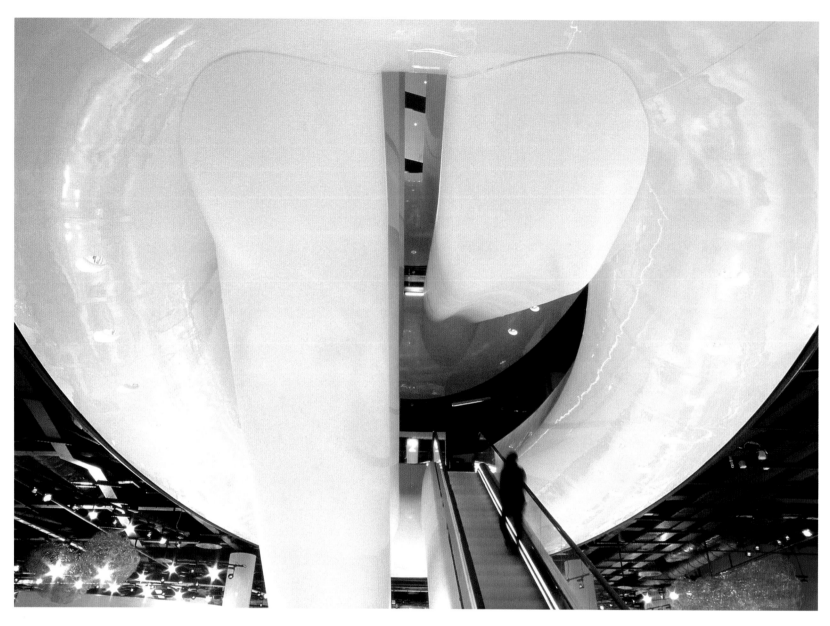

Opposite, top: The atrium, enclosed by lustrous white fiberglass, is a neutral unifier of the disparate floor designs.

Opposite, bottom left: Escalators crisscross the smaller of two atriums.

Opposite, bottom right: Future Systems designed the ground-floor food hall.

Left: Future Systems designed the ground-floor retail spaces, including the housewares department.

Following pages: Sinuous fiberglass balustrades and escalator casings define a cool, luminous atrium beneath a large skylight, one of two such spaces designed by Future Systems.

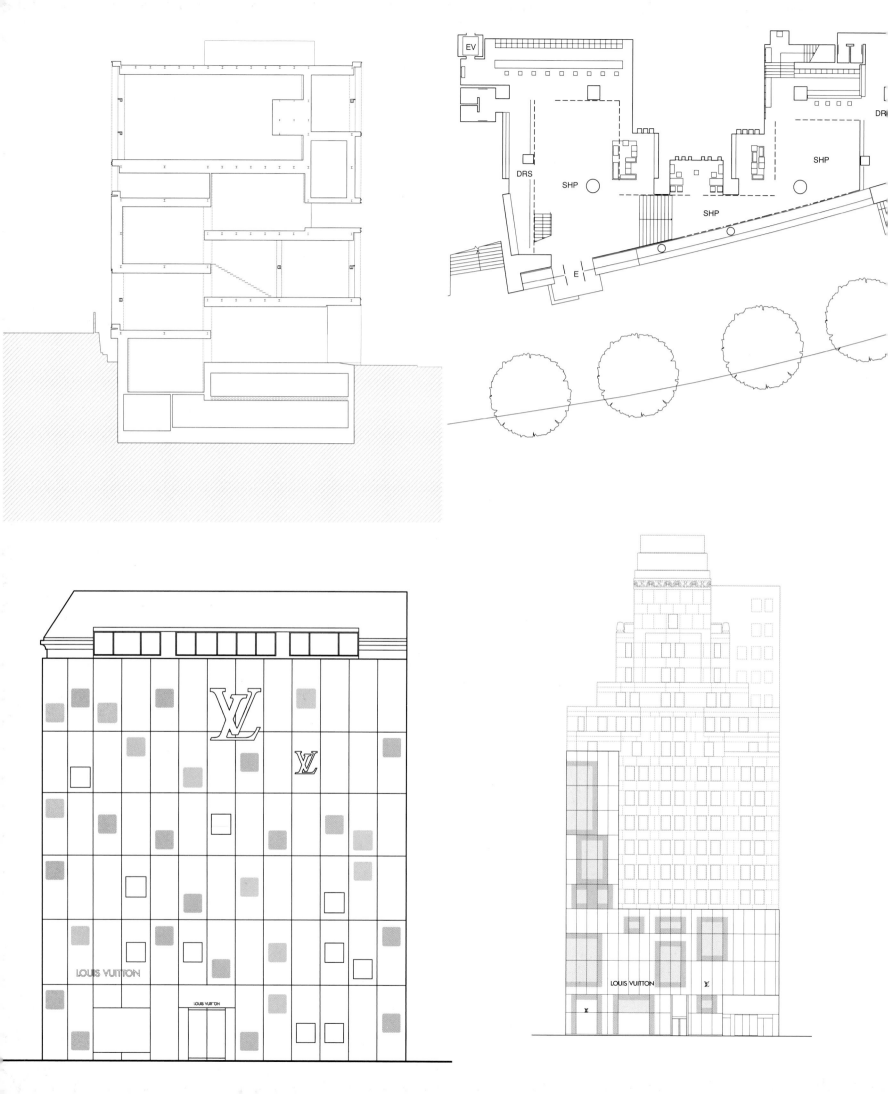

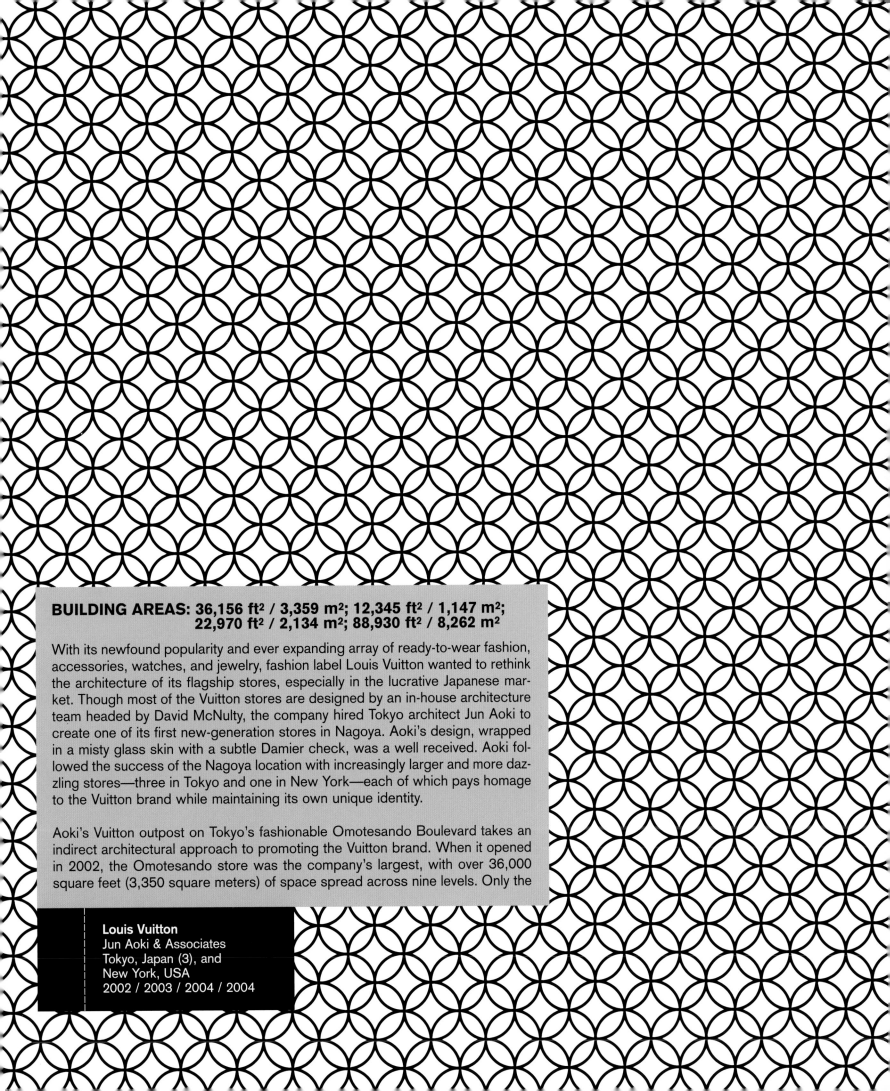

BUILDING AREAS: 36,156 ft² / 3,359 m²; 12,345 ft² / 1,147 m²; 22,970 ft² / 2,134 m²; 88,930 ft² / 8,262 m²

With its newfound popularity and ever expanding array of ready-to-wear fashion, accessories, watches, and jewelry, fashion label Louis Vuitton wanted to rethink the architecture of its flagship stores, especially in the lucrative Japanese market. Though most of the Vuitton stores are designed by an in-house architecture team headed by David McNulty, the company hired Tokyo architect Jun Aoki to create one of its first new-generation stores in Nagoya. Aoki's design, wrapped in a misty glass skin with a subtle Damier check, was a well received. Aoki followed the success of the Nagoya location with increasingly larger and more dazzling stores—three in Tokyo and one in New York—each of which pays homage to the Vuitton brand while maintaining its own unique identity.

Aoki's Vuitton outpost on Tokyo's fashionable Omotesando Boulevard takes an indirect architectural approach to promoting the Vuitton brand. When it opened in 2002, the Omotesando store was the company's largest, with over 36,000 square feet (3,350 square meters) of space spread across nine levels. Only the

Louis Vuitton
Jun Aoki & Associates
Tokyo, Japan (3), and
New York, USA
2002 / 2003 / 2004 / 2004

lower four floors are given over to retail and accessible to the public; the upper levels contain offices, a VIP lounge, and an event hall for fashion shows and product launches. Aoki treated the Omotesando store as a three-dimensional sculpture inspired by a pile of stacked Vuitton trunks. Each rectilinear box is sheathed in a luminous skin of tinted, polished stainless steel and glass layered with different patterns of wire mesh reminiscent of well-known Vuitton patterns. (There is one area, for instance, with a classic Vuitton checkerboard texture.) Inside, Vuitton's in-house design team created luxurious spaces that echo the metallic veils of Aoki's architecture.

Another Tokyo branch, designed by Aoki in the glittering new Roppongi Hills retail, office, and entertainment complex, sets

itself apart with a striking, mysterious facade of horizontal glass tubes and perforated stainless steel. Aoki worked with Italian architect Aurelio Clementi, Eric Carlson, and Vuitton's architecture studio on the overall design of the branch. Giant letters behind the 120-foot-long (37-meter-long) glass screen announce the Louis Vuitton name simply and elegantly. Inside the roughly 12,000-square-foot (1,100-square meter) store, Aoki and his collaborators reinterpreted Vuitton's vintage floral and circle-and-diamond patterns as crisp metal rings woven together into huge screens that separate retail areas without solid walls and cover surfaces in a hard-edged metal skin.

The store Aoki designed on Namiki Dori in Tokyo's Ginza area is perhaps the most direct and simple embodiment of the

Opposite: The stacked boxy profile of Vuitton Omotesando suggests the fashion house's signature trunks piled atop one another. Above: Aoki clad the exterior volumes of the store in a layered skin of glass-and-metal mesh, as well as rose- and gold-tinted polished stainless steel.

Above: A stacked display of vintage trunks from the Vuitton Museum in France reinforces the concept of the Omotesando store's exterior facade.
Opposite: Screens of glass and woven metal create delicate veils within the store.
Following pages: Aoki covered an upper-level hallway in patterned wood marquetry (left). The glass-and-metal-mesh exterior skin creates luminous, delicately veiled spaces inside the Omotesando shop. Like trunks of different sizes and shapes, the store's interiors vary from double height to low-ceilinged and intimate (right).

approach to translating Vuitton's patterns into architecture. The six-story corner shop is itself a square, blocky building. Aoki wrapped its exterior in a translucent white skin screened with squares of varying sizes along with square windows and door openings, all of which play on the Damier pattern. In the evening, the building turns into a glittering explosion of pattern and light: The facades reveal a random pattern of backlit squares, some plain, others composed of dozens of tinier squares. The *LV* monogram also makes an appearance. Inside, the geometry of display cases, mirrors, and video screens continue the exterior geometry.

The opening of Vuitton's New York flagship in 2004 coincided with the brand's 150th anniversary and became the setting

for a star-studded opening party. Aoki redesigned part of the exterior of the building, a 1930s structure that originally housed the New York Trust Company, while Manhattan architect Peter Marino took care of the three-story interior. On the outside, Aoki returned to the Damier check, which appears subtly in a skin of milky white glass that veils the building's large window openings. Inside, Marino continued the motif with gridded display cases—some with vintage Vuitton trunks above them—and, most obviously, in the illuminated LED wall that flanks the staircase linking the store's three levels of retail.

Aoki's variations on Vuitton's cherished logos successfully make the leap from steamer trunk to architecture. He interprets the patterns loosely enough that they can vary from building to

Opposite: The exterior of the Roppongi Hills store features a bold facade of stacked glass tubes with the Louis Vuitton name screened behind it.
Above: The lower reaches of display windows in the store feature layered metal rings that recall Vuitton's patterned logo.

Above and opposite: Screens of patterned metal rings extend throughout the interior of the Roppongi Hills location, creating partitions between different areas of the store.

building without becoming repetitive. For those who don't appreciate the references to checkerboards or four-leaf flowers, Aoki's graphics make attractive surface treatments. For those who do understand the symbolism, it reinforces the value of the Vuitton brand. Aoki's many projects for Vuitton display a synergy between architecture and retail—the buildings he creates support the brand without overwhelming it.

Above: The Louis Vuitton store on Namiki Dori in Tokyo's Ginza district appears as a solid white box dotted with a few square windows and doorways.
Opposite: At night, the illuminated interior reveals a random pattern of square windows and tiny punctures in the translucent skin, including the signature Louis Vuitton monogram logo.
Following pages: The square openings confound the viewer's sense of scale, as they make the six-story building appear much taller (left).
The interior is more conventional, with low ceilings and square walls and display vitrines that continue the exterior patterning inside (right).

Opposite: The Vuitton flagship in New York occupies a prime intersection in the Manhattan retail universe: the corner of Fifth Avenue and East Fifty-Seventh Street. Aoki created optical effects with the translucent white glass skin that faintly replicates Vuitton's checkerboard Damier leather pattern.

Left: At night, Vuitton's floors glow through broad windows extending up the corner of the historic 1930s New York Trust building.

Opposite: The centerpiece of the interior, designed by New York architect Peter Marino, is a multi-story LED wall that can render Vuitton's gridded Damier-inspired checkerboard pattern in dozens of different colors of light.
Above: Most of the display cases play off the gridded square pattern of the exterior glass. Vintage Vuitton trunks and hat boxes dot the interior decoration.

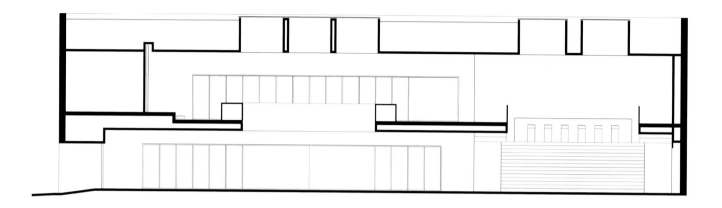

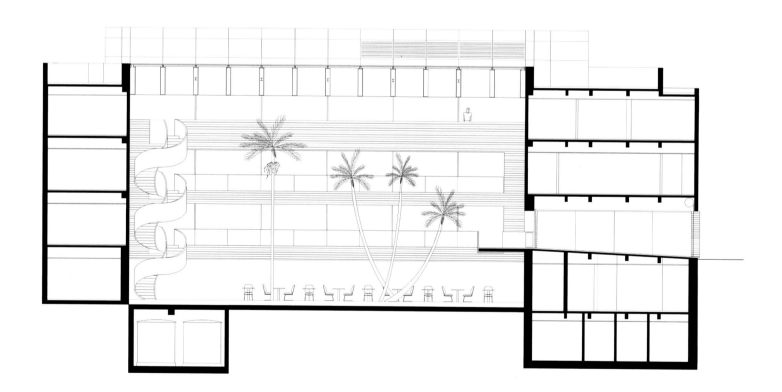

Forum and Clube Chocolate
Isay Weinfeld
São Paulo, Brazil
2001 / 2004

BUILDING AREA: 12,205 ft²; 1,114 m² / 18,665 ft²; 1,734 m²

Tufi Duek, the stylist and fashion designer who owns the trendy Brazilian clothing label Forum, hired architect Isay Weinfeld to design his flagship on São Paulo's fashionable Rua Oscar Freiere. Duek asked Weinfeld, who loves juxtaposing minimalism with humble materials to create surprisingly overscaled and dramatic interiors, to give architectural form to the themes that inspire his clothing. Among Duek's Brazilian muses are bossa nova, Cinema Novo, the beaches of Rio de Janeiro, and exotic tropical fruit. That might sound like a recipe for Carmen Miranda kitsch, but what Weinfeld delivered is a subtle, sophisticated blend of stark, whitewashed interiors and native Brazilian craft.

There are two entrances to the store, one through the women's area and one through the men's. Both of these areas are narrow, whitewashed spaces with clothing displays kept out of the way and clutter free with built-in racks illuminated by recessed lighting. That opens up the centers of the long, narrow volumes to sitting areas furnished with stylish midcentury Brazilian chairs juxtaposed with woven rag rugs typical of the country's northeast region.

Above left: One of two entrances to Forum, recessed into a textured stone wall.
Above right: At the center of the store, where separate wings for men's and women's clothing intersect, is a skylit double-height space.
Opposite: At one side of the towering atrium is a dramatic staircase wrapped in vitrified red glass tiles leading to a coffee bar, with a backdrop of rough *taipa*, a native Brazilian construction material.

The men's and women's zones intersect at the dramatic heart of the store, a towering skylit volume with the only splash of color in the otherwise all-white interior. (Weinfeld claims that color interferes with clothing.) Here, a broad staircase, covered in small lipstick-red glass tiles, leads to a wall covered in *taipa*, a rough material used to build modest homes in northern Brazil. In front of the textured gray wall is a long wood-topped coffee bar with stools made of tree trunks and upholstered in cowhide. The effect is spectacular, a powerful punch of color, texture, and handcrafted native materials that ground an otherwise neutral space in Brazil's rich tradition of craft.

Weinfeld's design for Clube Chocolate, a "lifestyle" store in the vein of Colette in Paris, is an even more literal evocation of the sultry sands of Ipanema and Copacabana. He constructed a beach inside the building. Located just down the street from Forum, Clube Chocolate has a similarly muted entry facade: a small square cutout in a solid wall of mustard-colored concrete. The square entry opens into a long, wood-lined corridor with a vitrine along one side that surreptitiously leads shoppers to the big surprise: a four-story skylit atrium filled with towering palm trees rising from a sandy bottom. A sleek spiral staircase wrapped in stainless steel winds up from the interior beach, the focal point of a café on the bottom level, joining the four floors of retail. The beach is an important part of Brazil's culture and social life; now shoppers in São Paulo, a landlocked concrete jungle of more than sixteen million residents, have the luxury of beachside café seating.

In typical Weinfeld fashion, the shop's material palette is a mix of the cool and the sensual, the abstract and the textural. Inside the atrium, the smooth polished steel enclosing the spiral stairs contrasts with the wall of rough pebbles set into concrete (the same mosaic technique used in Rio's famous patterned sidewalks) immediately behind it. Floors and ceilings of rich *peroba clara* wood from Brazil play against balustrades of glass and the exposed cables from which the floor levels hang. And, of course, all the architecture strikes a balance with the swath of sand and tropical foliage Weinfeld brought into the space. He is a master of cinematic interiors—the ideal architect for drama-hungry followers of fashion.

Opposite: Lounges within the shopping areas include armchairs by midcentury Brazilian designers and woven rag rugs from northern Brazil.
Left: Skylights bring daylight into display areas on the second floor.
Top right: The second floor includes areas for sportswear, dressing rooms, and an haute-couture salon.
Above right: Weinfeld kept display cases built into the walls to minimize visual clutter in the all-white space.

Opposite: The entry to the store is a discrete square opening punched into a smooth wall of mustard-colored concrete.

Top: A wood-lined corridor leads to the four-story atrium at the back of Clube Chocolate.

Left: Towering palm trees rise from an internal beach in the four-level atrium, flanked by a rough wall of stone.

Above: Glass balustrades open up views of the palm-filled courtyard from the shopping levels.
Opposite: A shiny spiral staircase wrapped in stainless steel winds up from the interior beach, overlooked by a café at the basement level, to the three above-grade shopping levels.

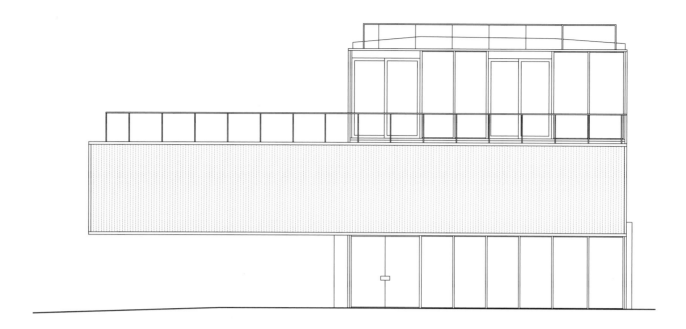

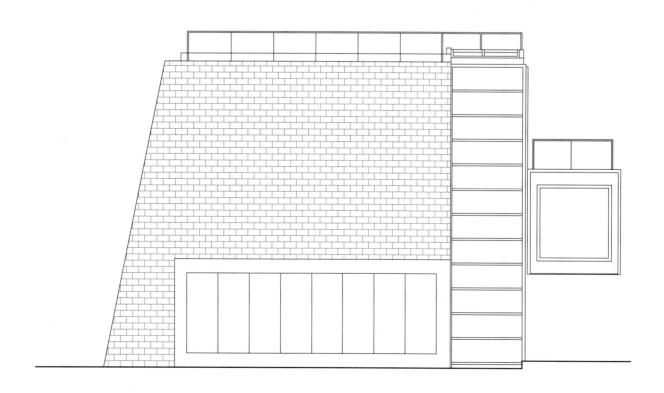

Undercover Lab
Klein Dytham architecture
Tokyo, Japan
2001

BUILDING AREA: 6,878 ft² / 639 m²

The Italian- and English-born, London-trained architects Astrid Klein and Mark Dytham established the design practice Klein Dytham architecture in Tokyo in 1991. The two went to Japan on a three-month tour and stayed on indefinitely because, as they say, there were too many "wild, weird, and wonderful things to see." Using innovative materials, technology, color, and humor to rethink their commissions, Klein and Dytham blend the best of East and West and draw on the constant Japanese thirst for discovering what's new. Their built projects include cutting-edge installations at the Laforet department store in Tokyo and a wedding chapel in the foothills of Japan's southern alps.

Klein and Dytham's design for Undercover Lab in Tokyo, a studio, showroom, press office, and warehouse for fashion designer Jun Takahashi, is tucked away among the narrow backstreets of Tokyo's crowded Harajuku district. The client requested a building that was understated and almost unnoticeable. Indeed, their design is easy to overlook: a sixty-six-foot-long (twenty-meter-long) tube of black corrugated metal cantilevered thirty-three feet (ten meters) above a small, square

Above: The black corrugated-metal box containing fashion designer Jun Takahashi's press showroom cantilevers thirty-three feet (ten meters) over a long, narrow driveway. Opposite: A large square window at the end of the metal box offers a tantalizing glimpse of the clothes inside.

site at the end of a long, narrow driveway. The long box has a mysterious quality, vaguely reminiscent of a shipping container full of unknown goods. The daring cantilever energizes an otherwise simple scheme and gives the building some much-needed presence on the street, but it serves another, more basic functional purpose: The client needed to be able to park five cars on the site, which would have been impossible with columns supporting the underside of the box.

The floating black box attaches itself to a three-story brick structure housing a warehouse, a showroom, meeting rooms, and a design studio. The double-height studio has a lofty feeling, with a skylight bringing in natural light along a wall sheathed in wood planks. A glass wall encloses a stair hall that

leads up to the press showroom in the adjacent box structure so journalists coming to preview Takahashi's street-savvy fashions don't have to march through the working areas. Takahashi asked that the press room include sixty-six-foot-long (twenty-meter-long) hanging racks to accommodate all of the clothes for a single season's collection; the corrugated tube was the logical place for these long runs of clothing. There's not much else to the space, a low-ceilinged, open volume with a large square window at the street end.

Takahashi's studio is quite understated for a designer of edgy, avant-garde, sometimes punk-tinged fashion who has won Japan's biggest fashion prizes and operates thirty-one boutiques across the country. (He plans to expand his label to New

York, Paris, Rome, London, Hong Kong, and other fashion centers.) Then again, the name of his label, Under Cover, may be a misnomer. And while Klein Dytham pursued a stealthy, low-profile aesthetic, their design is striking nonetheless.

Opposite: The press showroom features display racks long enough to hold an entire season's fashions.
Above: One wall of the loftlike, double-height design studio is covered in wood decking.

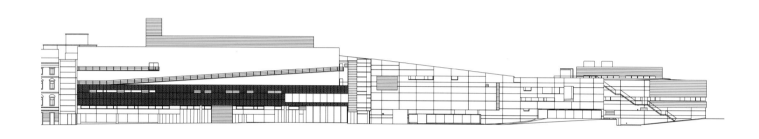

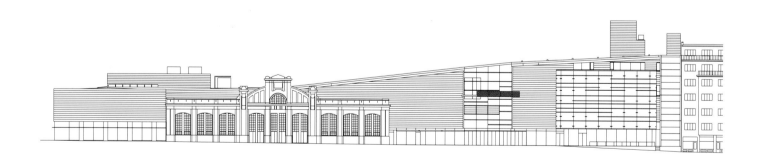

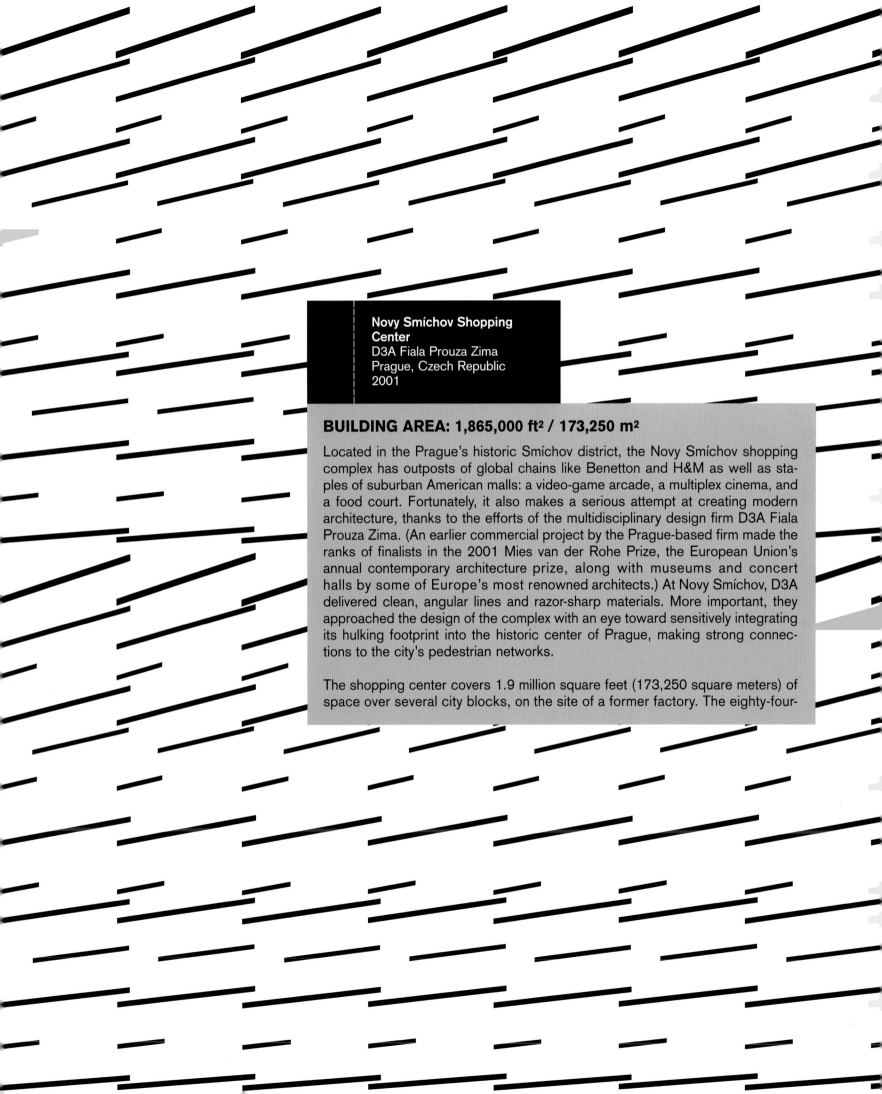

Novy Smíchov Shopping Center
D3A Fiala Prouza Zima
Prague, Czech Republic
2001

BUILDING AREA: 1,865,000 ft² / 173,250 m²

Located in the Prague's historic Smíchov district, the Novy Smíchov shopping complex has outposts of global chains like Benetton and H&M as well as staples of suburban American malls: a video-game arcade, a multiplex cinema, and a food court. Fortunately, it also makes a serious attempt at creating modern architecture, thanks to the efforts of the multidisciplinary design firm D3A Fiala Prouza Zima. (An earlier commercial project by the Prague-based firm made the ranks of finalists in the 2001 Mies van der Rohe Prize, the European Union's annual contemporary architecture prize, along with museums and concert halls by some of Europe's most renowned architects.) At Novy Smíchov, D3A delivered clean, angular lines and razor-sharp materials. More important, they approached the design of the complex with an eye toward sensitively integrating its hulking footprint into the historic center of Prague, making strong connections to the city's pedestrian networks.

The shopping center covers 1.9 million square feet (173,250 square meters) of space over several city blocks, on the site of a former factory. The eighty-four-

Above left: Concrete and glass are the primary building materials.

Above right: An elevated walkway pierces a concrete retaining wall, which links the shopping center with existing pedestrian paths through the city.

Opposite: Much of the shopping center's bulk is disguised with a curved, grass-covered wall. Ventilation grilles create an abstract pattern on the grassy facade.

million-dollar project includes three levels of parking for two-thousand cars, shops, a twelve-screen cinema multiplex, cafés, restaurants, and the anchor tenant, an outpost of the French hypermarket chain Carrefour.

On the outside, the sprawling complex seems well designed but slightly generic. The main entrance, along the south facade, opens onto a plaza set back from the street. The six-story-high exterior features taut, crisply detailed walls of titanium and glass that rise in height to negotiate the different scales of adjoining buildings. The north elevation is more dynamic, with a black base animated by bands of tinted glass windows and an exterior walkway extending along the upper reaches of the angular concrete structure. The project's real strength is in the weaving

of such a vast program into the urban fabric of Prague without being either obtrusive or garish.

The most dramatic resolution is along the shopping center's western side, where the architects diminished the visual bulk of the structure by covering the exterior in a curving, grass-covered wall. Ventilation grilles punched into the grassy surface—it's far too steep to be considered a natural hillside in the middle of the city—create a surreal pattern of "windows." This unexpected patch of nature works well in creating an unobtrusive backdrop to an existing historic building at the corner of the site. Even more notable is how the architects handled circulation into and through the site. Rather than drop an enormous self-contained and hermetically sealed building into the

Above: At the northwest corner of the building, angular catwalks animate the solid reaches of the facade.

Opposite: The retail mix includes smaller shops and the French hypermarket chain Carrefour.

middle of Prague's medieval streets, they sliced walkways and passages into its large footprint. For instance, a 650-foot-long (200-meter-long) passageway extends through the middle of the shopping center, the deepest part of the floor plate. An elevated pedestrian bridge feeds into the western face of the mall to provide access from residential areas of the city.

Providing multiple points of entry into such a sprawling shopping enclave is as much about tying it into the city as it is about providing more entrances for shoppers to get to the merchandise. Although it possesses some of the worst elements of suburban malls, Novy Smíchov also captures some of the best ideas of traditional urban European shopping.

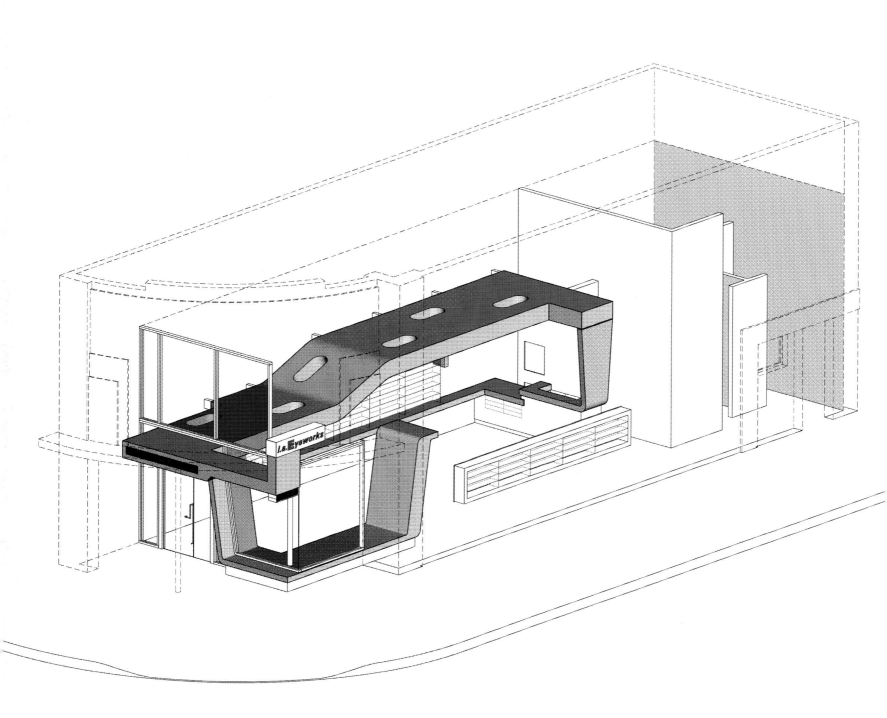

l.a. Eyeworks
Neil M. Denari Architects
Los Angeles, USA
2003

BUILDING AREA: 1,150 ft² / 107 m²

The eyewear company l.a. Eyeworks did much to make spectacles and sunglasses fashionable in the United States. Founded in the 1970s by Gai Gherardi and Barbara McReynolds, the company launched ad campaigns with edgy pop icons like Boy George and RuPaul wearing their designs, accompanied by the tagline, "A face is like a work of art. It deserves a great frame." In real life, the likes of Mick Jagger, artist Chuck Close, and actress Susan Sarandon have made l.a. Eyeworks frames desirable to not-so-famous but stylish faces everywhere.

McReynolds and Gherardi hired Los Angeles architect Neil Denari to design a 1,150-square-foot (107-square-meter) flagship store on Beverly Boulevard in West Hollywood. The company has other retail outposts, but this high-profile location is reserved for in-house designs. Denari, the former director of the influential Los Angeles architecture school SCI-Arc, transformed a former storage building with a prominent curved corner into a cool, watery blue space. Except for the exterior bull-nose curve, the shop would have been a long, narrow space with a tiny storefront. Denari turned it into a dynamic composition of intersecting

Previous pages: An LED text display merges visually into a suspended drywall canopy that extends toward the back of the store (left). The square display window contrasts with the rounded corner of the existing building. The shop's interior includes a long mirrored display case beneath the drywall canopy, punctuated with circular and elliptical openings (right).

geometries, undulating surfaces, and movable furniture that rivals the hip design of McReynolds and Gherardi's frames.

On the exterior, Denari slipped a square display window beneath the curved stucco of the existing facade. A low plaster-covered bench along the base of the window curves up at an angle and intersects a boxy canopy with an LED screen displaying text messages above the door. The canopy surrounding the digital display extends out beyond the curving facade, where it intersects another sign featuring the store's logo and street address.

Denari blurred the boundaries between interior and exterior space by visually pulling the exterior canopy inside, where it

becomes a suspended plane floating beneath the ceiling. As it extends toward the cash-wrap desk at the back of the shop, the canopy folds upward to create a topographically varied plane that curves from eight up to ten feet above the terrazzo floor. Circular lights pop out from the canopy; elliptical cutouts in the drywall surface are backlit to suggest a pattern of tiny skylights.

The eyeglasses are displayed on opposite walls. One unit, wrapped in a thick frame of painted fiberboard, stacks frames on four shelves with a mirrored background so customers can try on options themselves. The other display case is wrapped in an aluminum frame; behind it is a wall of polystyrene squares, a lively graphic installation by artist Jim Isermann that plays

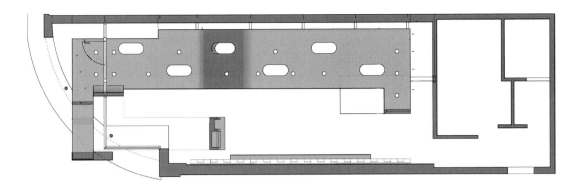

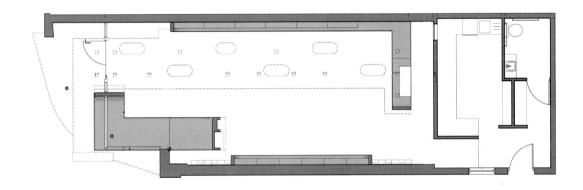

against the smooth surfaces of Denari's architecture. Except for Isermann's gridded wall, the entire space is a wash of cool, icy blue. With so much blue around it, the wall sculpture also takes on a subtle reflected tint.

Denari designed the tables where customers are fitted with frames as movable pieces of furniture on casters. During the day, the stainless-steel and acrylic tables with composite tops are the only objects occupying the center of the long, narrow floor; at night, they can be rolled away to maintain the shop's clean lines. As with l.a. Eyeworks' frames, Denari's design is as much about the overall gesture as it is about the precision of the details.

Opposite: Denari designed the desks where customers are fitted with glasses as angular stainless-steel and polycarbonate furniture that can be moved around the store on casters.
Above: Ceiling plan (top); floor plan (bottom).

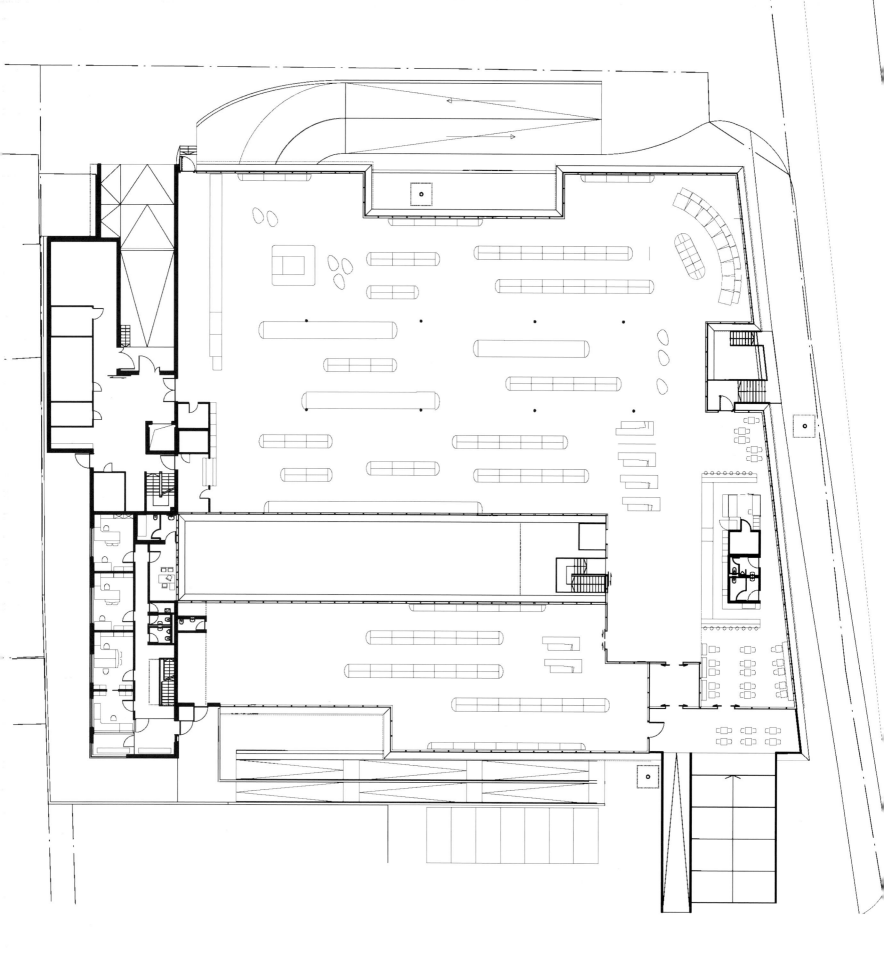

BUILDING AREA: 57,015 ft² / 5,297 m²

The most internationally recognized architect to design a branch of the MPreis chain is Parisian Dominique Perrault, responsible for such projects as the Olympic Velodrome in Berlin and, most famously, the Bibliothèque nationale de France, in Paris. He has also designed three supermarkets for MPreis: one in Zirl, Austria, and two in Wattens, east of Innsbruck. All three structures capture Perrault's minimalist aesthetic of crisply detailed glass and ethereal scrims of perforated metals, and all of them integrate clean, high-tech architecture with the spectacular surroundings of the Austrian Alps.

Perrault's second MPreis location in Wattens (population 7,300) sits directly on one of the town's main streets. The 34,480-square-foot (3,205-square-meter) market fronts a small paved plaza along the street giving the building a distinctly urban feeling. (A towering sign with a large "Super M" logo looks like a giant marker for a subway station.) As in other MPreis locations, Perrault raised the single-story structure on concrete columns to slip the car park beneath the building, thereby eliminating the sea of parking that surrounds most conventional

MPreis Supermarket
Dominique Perrault Architecte
Wattens, Austria
2003

Previous pages: The market's main entrance fronts a small plaza.
Above: Perforated metal skins partially screen the glass facades from the adjacent road.

supermarkets. In this case, Perrault took the parking scheme a step further, integrating landscape and parking in what he calls "green courts," narrow courtyards cut into the floor plan with trees growing between the building sections. The courtyards help break up the monotony of the large floor plate, adding additional surface area, which Perrault clad in glass to bring more daylight deep into the space. Offices, loading docks, and storage are located at the back of the store, away from the street side, where a small café occupies a corner adjoining the entry plaza.

Most of the market's facades are panes of glass extending from floor to ceiling. Perrault veiled some of the tall glass panes in shimmering screens of corrugated, perforated metal; others he

left uncovered, bringing tremendous amounts of natural light and large swaths of alpine scenery indoors. At night, the market becomes a giant light box as the illuminated interiors glow through both the clear and the thinly veiled facades.

Perrault's design does not reinvent the standardized box that has served supermarkets and other large-scale retailers well. It does, however, completely transform the experience of shopping in a big box. Tall, lofty ceilings, plenty of natural light, panoramic views of the Alps, and parking beneath trees in the middle of a courtyard—nothing about the MPreis experience is off-the-shelf. With minimal means, Perrault's design adds great value to the MPreis brand.

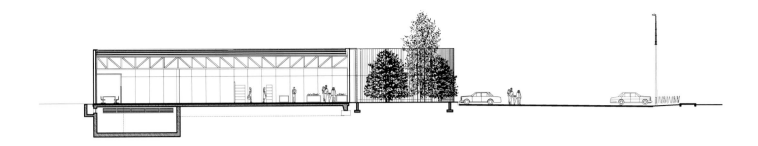

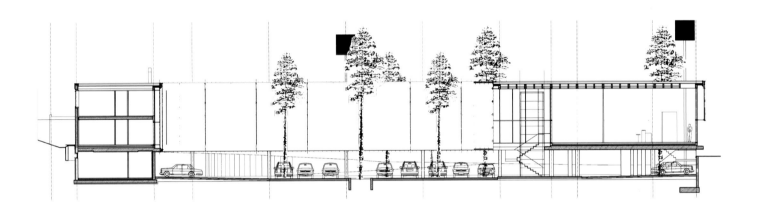

Above: Sections reveal the integration of landscape, parking, and building.

Following pages, clockwise from top left: Tall
ceilings and walls of floor-to-ceiling glass give
the supermarket interior a lofty feel. Shelving
maintains views of the surrounding landscape
through the glass walls. Compact parking beneath
the elevated structure minimizes the sprawl
surrounding most supermarkets. Stairs between
two bays of the partially screened structure lead
to the covered parking.

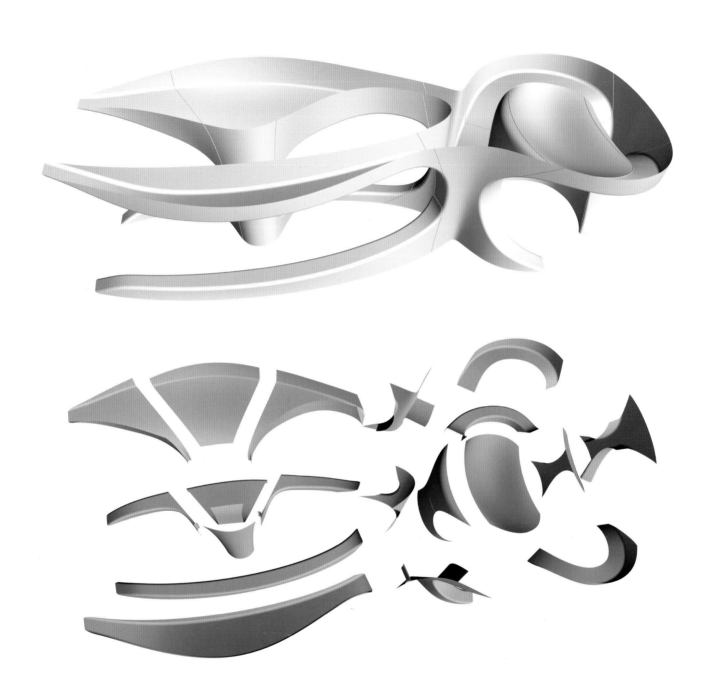

BUILDING AREA: 3,230 ft² / 300 m²

There's a long-standing debate over whether clothes should be displayed, like art, in a pure white box or in an environment that evokes the mood of the clothes or the image of the brand. Brazilian designer Carlos Miele chose the neutral option for the design of his first US store, in Manhattan's Meatpacking District. The São Paulo–based Miele is hardly afraid of color: His designs, loved by the Brazilian glitterati, include vibrant metallic frocks; flouncy, high-cut scarlet dresses; leather catsuits; and shaggy orange furs—perhaps all the more reason for an all-white store. Miele commissioned architects Hani Rashid and Lise-Anne Couture of the New York firm Asymptote to design a fluid, whitewashed store that creates a neutral but assertive backdrop for his clothes.

Rashid and Couture, known for sinuous computer-generated forms, found geometric inspiration in fabric scraps found on the floor of Miele's studio. Using the computer, they translated the shape of those scraps, along with the sensuous curves of the human body, into an organically shaped spine that extends down the center of the store. The sculptural spine, constructed of bent plywood

Carlos Miele Flagship
Asymptote
New York, USA
2003

Left: Mannequins float above a glass-covered ring of lighting embedded in the reflective floor, finished in two shades of epoxy. A sculptural construction through the center of the store doubles as seating and display surfaces.

covered in a glossy lacquer, functions both as a dramatic display unit and as seating. Rashid and Couture had the irregularly-shaped fluid form laser cut from computer files used to create the working drawings.

The curving, seemingly liquid construction continues the fluid patterns and pale, reflective sheen of the store's floors, walls, and ceilings. The contoured, stretched-fabric ceiling, which bubbles around light fixtures, is finished in a high-gloss epoxy, as is the two-tone floor. Rings of light covered in tempered glass create uplit halos beneath mannequins that float above the floor on transparent wires extending from the ceiling. Along the perimeter walls, clothes hang from simple built-in racks above another landscape of ebbing and flowing white lacquer.

The similarities between Miele's colorful clothes and Asymptote's sinuous architecture are stronger than one might imagine. Despite its cool atmosphere, Rashid and Couture's design is as exuberant and baroque as some of Miele's outlandish fashions. The architects and fashion designer share an obvious concern for voluptuous curves, whether those of the human body or non-orthogonal space. Another point of kinship is the computer technology needed to translate Asymptote's sweeping curves into buildable reality and used to help create Miele's boldly patterned fabrics. Miele often explores high-tech textiles and innovative fabrics made from recycled materials. Neither his clothes nor Asymptote's architecture have an overtly technological look to them but that is part of the magic of suspending belief, whether in architecture or fashion.

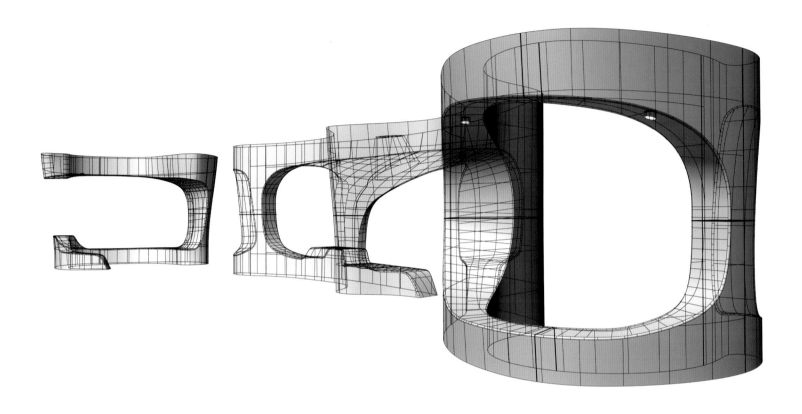

Opposite: The plain glass storefront along a gritty stretch of Manhattan's Meatpacking District reveals the shop's whitewashed interior.
Above: Asymptote designed the organically shaped display unit on the computer and used the digital files to laser-cut the lacquered plywood structure.
Following pages: Although the fluid interior landscape has its own strong identity, it lets Miele's clothes take center stage.

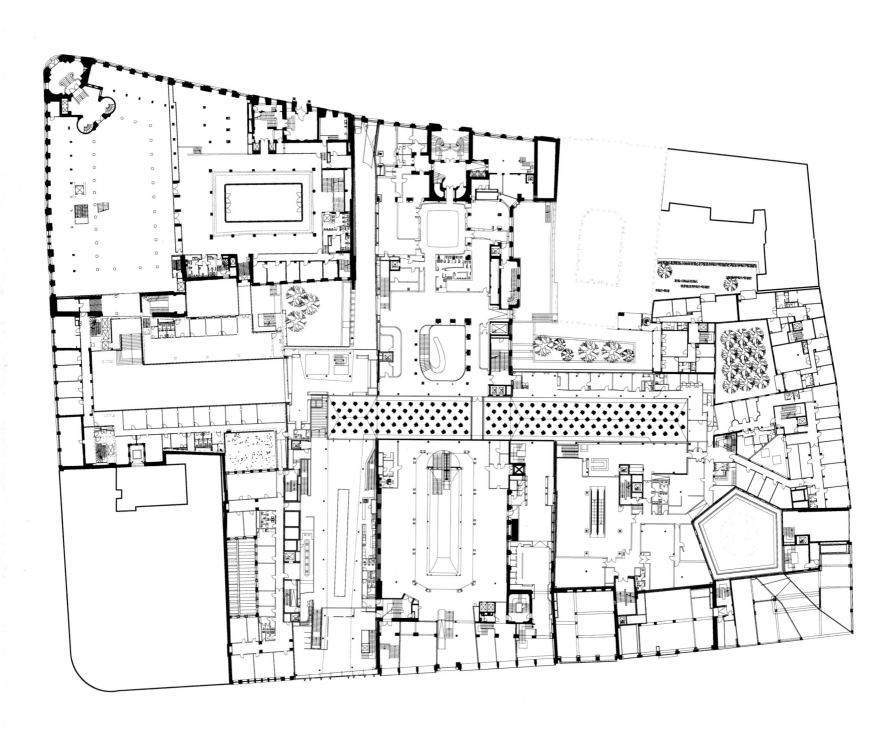

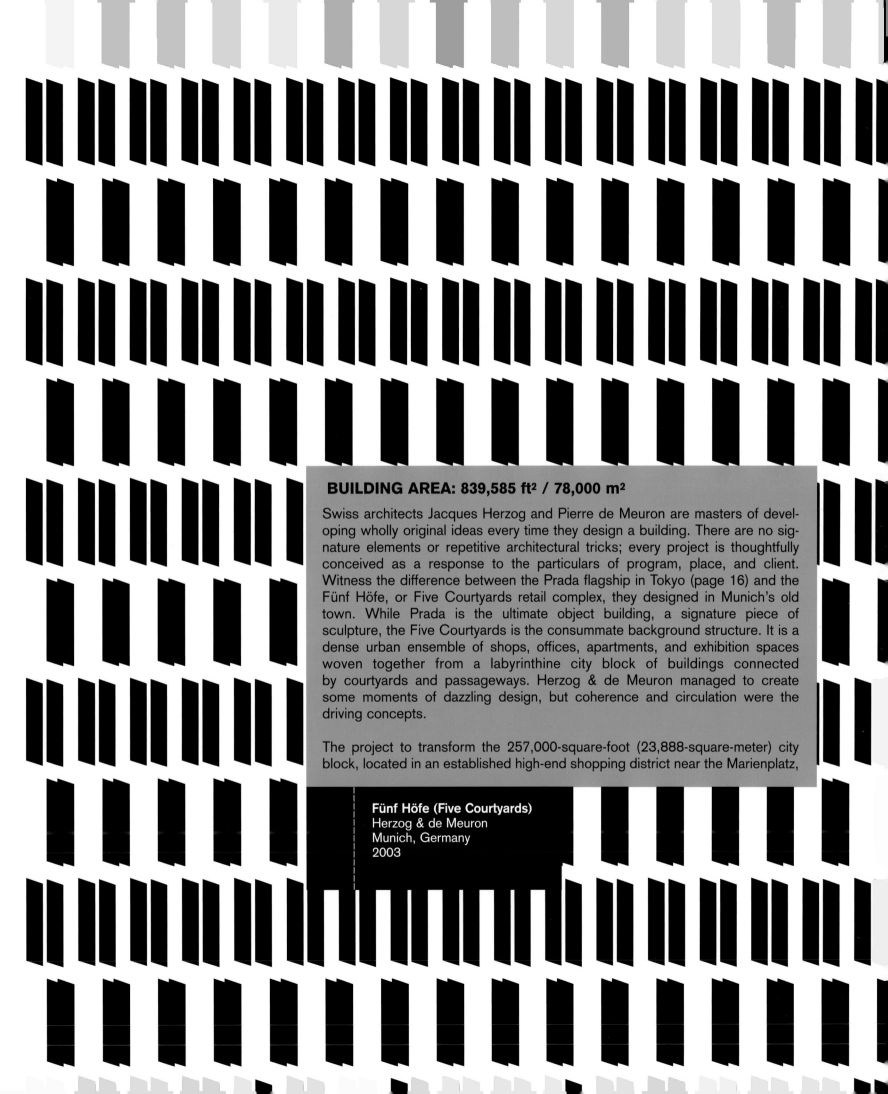

BUILDING AREA: 839,585 ft² / 78,000 m²

Swiss architects Jacques Herzog and Pierre de Meuron are masters of developing wholly original ideas every time they design a building. There are no signature elements or repetitive architectural tricks; every project is thoughtfully conceived as a response to the particulars of program, place, and client. Witness the difference between the Prada flagship in Tokyo (page 16) and the Fünf Höfe, or Five Courtyards retail complex, they designed in Munich's old town. While Prada is the ultimate object building, a signature piece of sculpture, the Five Courtyards is the consummate background structure. It is a dense urban ensemble of shops, offices, apartments, and exhibition spaces woven together from a labyrinthine city block of buildings connected by courtyards and passageways. Herzog & de Meuron managed to create some moments of dazzling design, but coherence and circulation were the driving concepts.

The project to transform the 257,000-square-foot (23,888-square-meter) city block, located in an established high-end shopping district near the Marienplatz,

Fünf Höfe (Five Courtyards)
Herzog & de Meuron
Munich, Germany
2003

into a retail complex was the brainchild of the banking conglomerate that co-owns the site. The program called for a mix of shops, restaurants, cafés, and a bank at street level, with an art gallery, offices, and apartments on the upper floors. The architects refer to their design as a European take on the American shopping mall, but in its comfortable mix of functions and its internalized sequence of internal arcades, passageways, and courtyards, the Five Courtyards is an inherently European vision of urban shopping, life, and culture.

The architects had to keep the existing facades along the perimeter of the block with only one exception; they added one new exterior, a four-story wing with two levels of retail topped with two office floors. Clad in operable shutters of bronze

mesh, the new facade puts a modern spin on the shuttered exteriors of neighboring structures.

Inside the block is where Herzog & de Meuron were able to work their magic. In reorganizing and refurbishing hallways and courtyards leading past baroque facades to shops such as Zara, Emporio Armani, and Dolce & Gabbana, the architects made surprising moments that thrill and delight shoppers with their unexpected variety. In one corner of the site, they covered a vaulted corridor in a scintillating pattern of iridescent glass tiles. An arcade leading from the street to one of the five courtyards is crowned with a hanging garden of thirty-three-foot-long (ten-meter-long) strands of ivy suspended from the ceiling, interspersed with glowing pendant lights. A reflective glass

Opposite: The only new street elevation in the Fünf Höfe complex features motorized bronze mesh shutters that shade offices above two levels of retail.

Above: Mirrored surfaces in an internal courtyard create complex reflections of bronze-shuttered office floors and a café attached to the *Kunsthalle*.

Top left: Playful orange tables in the *Kunsthalle* café overlook a retail passage below.

Above left: Artist Rémy Zaugg created richly radiant stair halls and elevator lobbies throughout the complex.

Above right: A functional hanging garden mixes dangling plants with a grid of pendant lights and hidden irrigation systems.

Opposite: Above a ground-level retail passageway sheathed in reflective glass, a glass roof opens up views of the bronze-shuttered office wing.

curtain wall cladding the shops along another arcade creates a fun house–like series of reflections.

While Herzog & de Meuron did not design the retail interiors, they created a unique space for retail outlets to establish stores and collaborated with artists to enliven the complex. Artist Rémy Zaugg illuminated elevator lobbies and stair halls with deep, moody colors to create abstract pauses in the Five Courtyards' eclectic palette. A giant metallic sphere fills a pentagonal courtyard at one corner of the site. And artist Thomas Ruff mounted photographic prints on a series of floor panels. There is also a *Kunsthalle* with 11,834 square feet (1,100 square meters) of exhibition space divided between two of the buildings in the complex.

Herzog & de Meuron took the right approach to an unwieldy program: They let variety shine through as they wove together buildings and spaces of different sizes, styles, and functions into a lively whole. Unlike the sanitized American mall, this European shopping precinct celebrates the messy vitality of urban life.

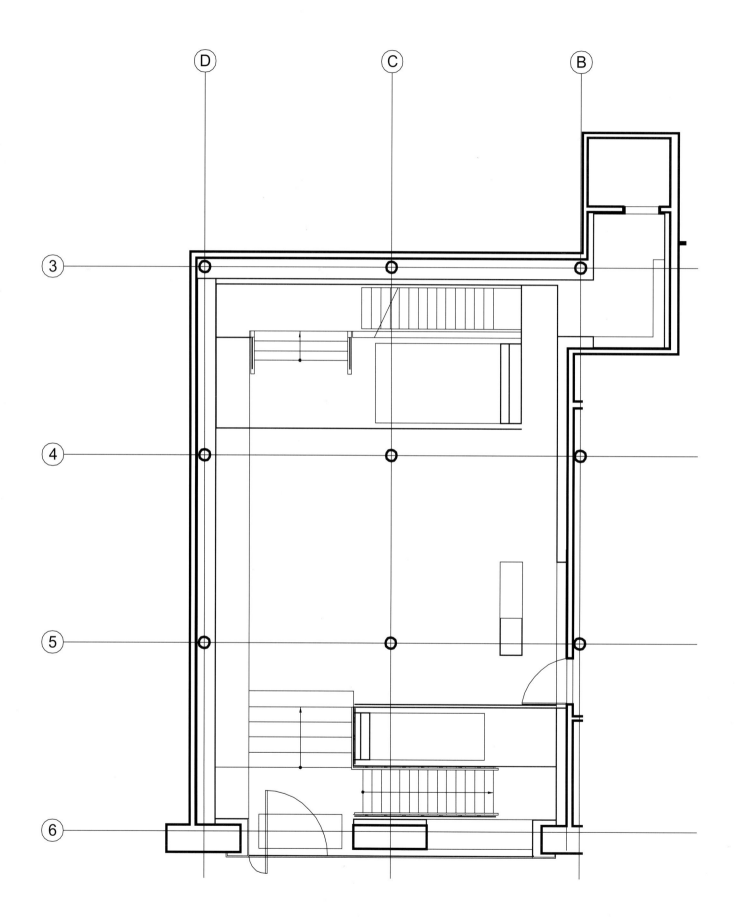

BUILDING AREA: 13,000 ft² / 1,208 m²

The Swiss furniture manufacturer Vitra has made commissioning the world's top architects an important part of its identity. At Vitra's main corporate campus in Weil am Rhein, Germany, Antonio Citterio, Nicholas Grimshaw, and Alvaro Siza designed factory buildings; Tadao Ando created a conference center; Zaha Hadid built her first project, a fire station; and Frank Gehry created a design museum. Vitra's CEO, Rolf Fehlbaum, has galvanized the company's commitment to cutting-edge architecture. Therefore, it might be slightly surprising that he hired a virtually unknown architect to design Vitra's New York showroom and headquarters in the burgeoning Meatpacking District.

Before being hired by Vitra, South African–born architect Lindy Roy of the New York–based firm ROY had built only a temporary art installation. Fehlbaum considered more established but still provocative designers such as Rem Koolhaas, Herzog & de Meuron, and Diller + Scofidio but wanted to invest in the promise of a younger talent like Roy. After all, Hadid hadn't built a building before being tapped to design Vitra's Weil am Rhein fire station, which opened in 1993.

Vitra
ROY
New York, USA
2004

Above: The only solid element along the transparent street facade is a backlit sign with the company's logo; Vitra's signature furniture is the primary attraction.

Opposite, top: The contract-furniture showroom and offices on the second floor are a bright, open space.

Opposite, bottom: A curved display element extends into the basement-level gallery space.

Roy transformed three levels of a heavy nineteenth-century brick warehouse into a visually light, energetic showcase for Vitra's classic designs by the likes of Jean Prouvé, Verner Panton, and Charles and Ray Eames, as well as younger talents such as Jasper Morrison and the Bouroullec brothers from Paris. The 13,000-square-foot (1,208-square-meter) project includes showroom space on the street level and on a much larger second floor, which also has offices, and a basement level for changing design exhibitions. On the outside, Roy simply inserted a clear glass skin into the masonry facade to make the showroom part of the streetscape. Inside, she cut away slices in the concrete floors to blur divisions between spaces and introduced a ribbon of rubber and steel that visually joins the three levels with what looks like a giant conveyor

belt transporting chairs from one floor to another. The continuous blending of floors, walls, counters, and staircases creates a lively flow of space in what is otherwise a simple, no-nonsense interior.

Although the Vitra store was her first built architecture project, Roy resisted the urge to overwhelm the space with her own pent-up ideas: She instead let her design take a backseat to Vitra's products, many of them works of art in their own right. Roy lined an entire wall of the ground-floor retail space with polycarbonate panels that she illuminated from behind to create a luminous backdrop. In front of the glowing wall, she added a simple slab on which chairs are displayed in single file, like a parade of design objects on view in a museum gallery.

Previous pages: A curving display element extends through openings between the three floors, creating visual continuity from the basement-level gallery to the second-floor offices. The display suggests a conveyor belt circulating classic Vitra chairs by Prouvé and Panton.

With merchandise as eye-popping as Vitra's collections, Roy's strategy is the right one. The space has enough personality and finesse to fit in with its larger architectural ambitions but is restrained enough to let the furniture shine. Roy's creation is a strong start to a promising career, and another example of Vitra's commitment to cutting-edge architecture.

Opposite and above: Roy kept the materials on the ground floor simple: rough concrete, wood, and a backlit wall of polycarbonate panels that put chairs by Jean Prouvé, Verner Panton, Frank Gehry, and other designers on display, as in a museum.

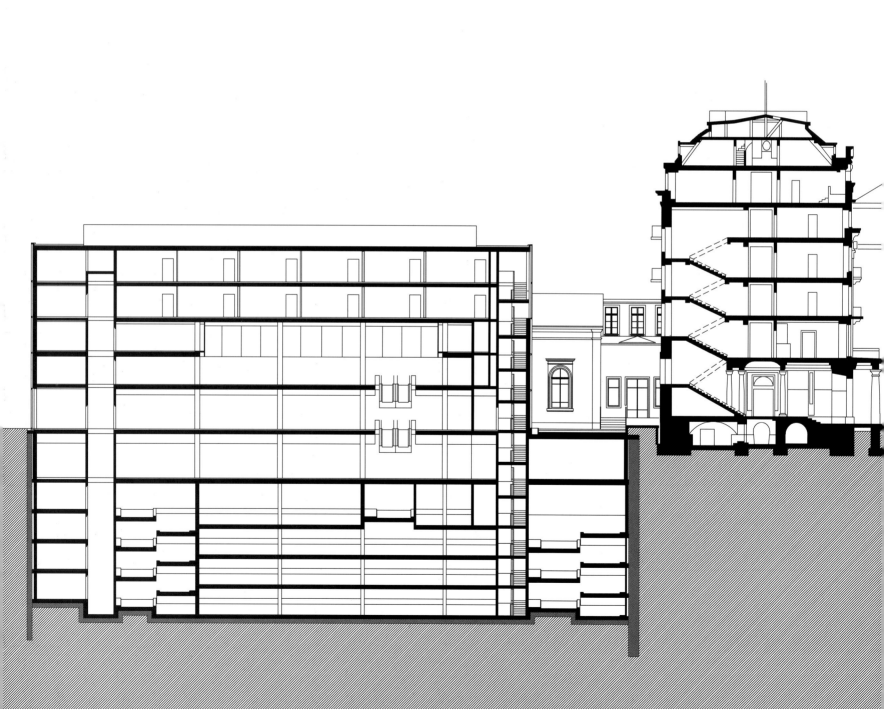

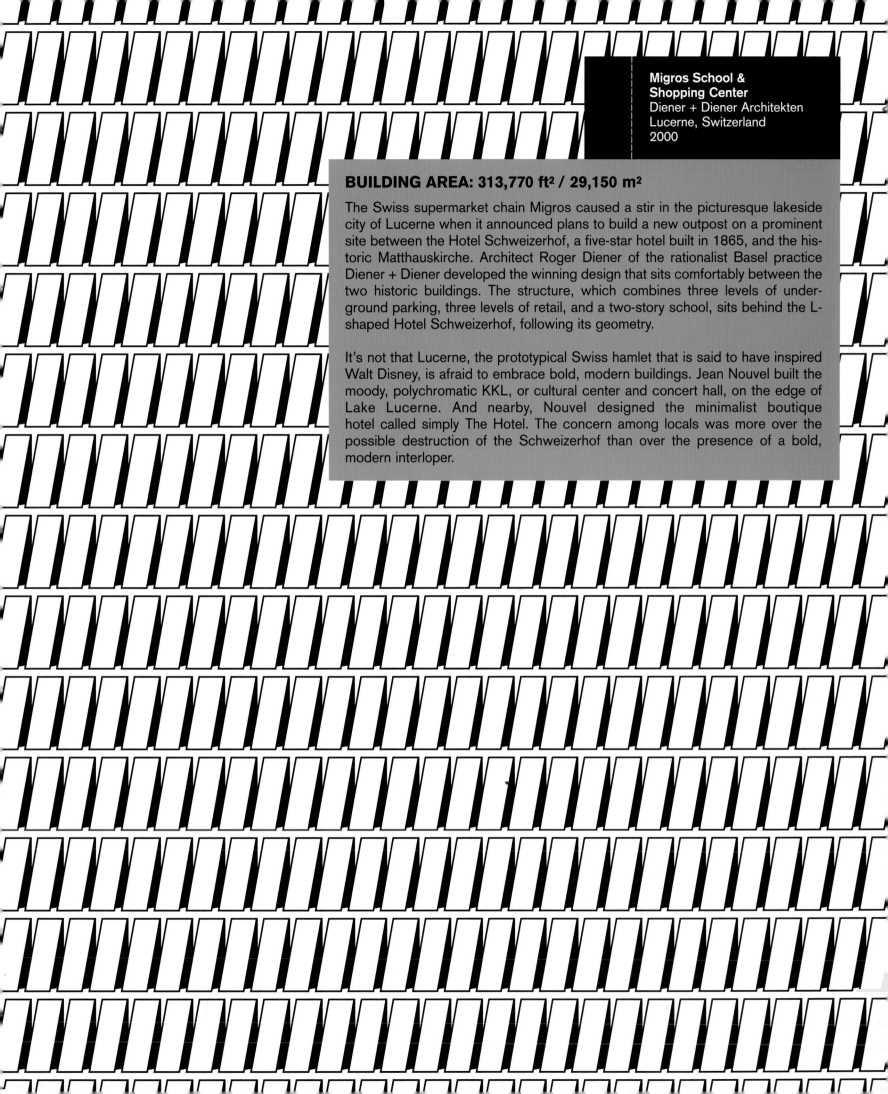

BUILDING AREA: 313,770 ft² / 29,150 m²

The Swiss supermarket chain Migros caused a stir in the picturesque lakeside city of Lucerne when it announced plans to build a new outpost on a prominent site between the Hotel Schweizerhof, a five-star hotel built in 1865, and the historic Matthauskirche. Architect Roger Diener of the rationalist Basel practice Diener + Diener developed the winning design that sits comfortably between the two historic buildings. The structure, which combines three levels of underground parking, three levels of retail, and a two-story school, sits behind the L-shaped Hotel Schweizerhof, following its geometry.

It's not that Lucerne, the prototypical Swiss hamlet that is said to have inspired Walt Disney, is afraid to embrace bold, modern buildings. Jean Nouvel built the moody, polychromatic KKL, or cultural center and concert hall, on the edge of Lake Lucerne. And nearby, Nouvel designed the minimalist boutique hotel called simply The Hotel. The concern among locals was more over the possible destruction of the Schweizerhof than over the presence of a bold, modern interloper.

Diener's building may not be an interloper, but it is indeed bold and modern. He took inspiration for the supermarket–cum–educational building from the church next door: He composed the exterior massing with the top two floors set back from the lower three levels to create a profile rather like the nave and side aisles of a church. Overall, the building is a simple, mono-lithic box; the neatly recessed upper floors constitute the only interruption in an otherwise taut block. Diener clad the solid parts of the facades in a grid of green-tinted oxidized-copper panels that clearly delineate the building's floor levels. He set fixed windows flush with the copper panels and picked a smoky green glass to create a unified, monolithic appearance. Diener clad the classrooms—located on the third, fourth, and fifth floors above grade—in alternating bands of fixed and

Left: The lower floors contain retail space; above is a school offering adult-education courses.
Above: Operable windows extend along the building's upper levels.

Above, left: The building sits on the historic steets of Lucerne but its modern design does not clash with the surrounding buildings.
Above, right: The smoky green glass of the windows echoes the color of the oxidized-copper panels cladding the exteriors.
Opposite: In a provocative juxtaposition of education and commerce, corridors of the Migros School overlook the shopping levels through internal walls of glass.

pivoting windows, also in a smoky tint to match the solid copper panels of the facades. The taut green skin gives the building a distinct profile among the gabled chalet-style buildings of the surrounding city.

The most interesting part of the project is the Migros School on the building's three uppermost levels. Migros operates the school as an adult-education venue, offering courses in foreign languages, computer technology, sports, cooking, music, and decorative arts. (Diener designed a separate building, located behind the hotel, that contains music classrooms and a gymnasium.) On the third level, classrooms are arranged along corridors wrapping the interior of the building that overlook the shopping area below through walls of floor-to-ceiling glass.

As students shuttle between classes, there is no forgetting the corporate nature of the Migros School or the interplay between education and commerce, between the acquisition of knowledge and the acquisition of merchandise.

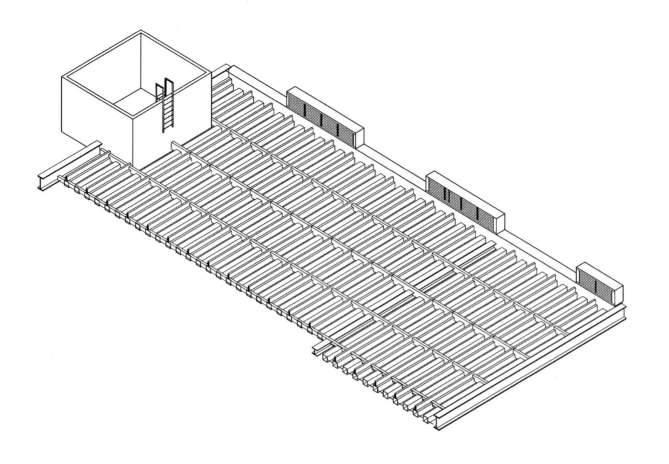

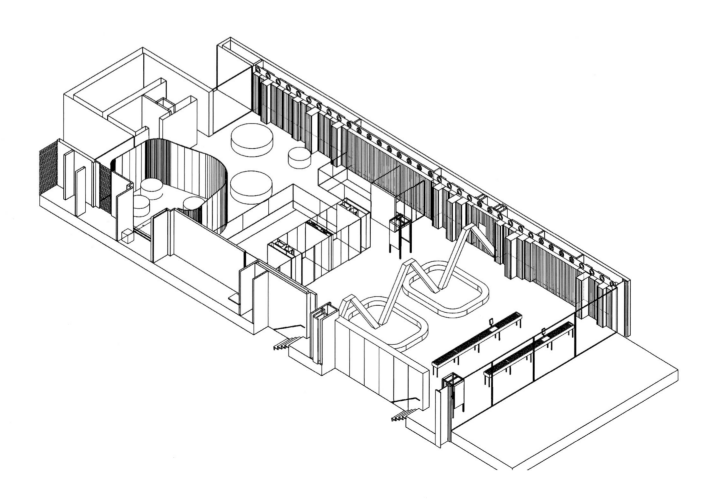

BUILDING AREA: 24,000 ft² / 2,230 m²

Rem Koolhaas's Prada Epicenter in Los Angeles covers 24,000 square feet (2,230 square meters) on three levels and a basement. The shop faces a palm-lined stretch of fabled Rodeo Drive in Beverly Hills, sandwiched between a Gucci store and Brioni. Koolhaas's architectural subversion begins immediately. There is no front door—there is, in fact, no street facade, just a forty-five-foot-wide (14-meter-wide) void. The architect purposely left the boundary between public and private space completely undefined. By day, the only separations between inside and outside are invisible: an air curtain for climate control and a security system with hidden antennas. At night, a huge aluminum grate rises from beneath the sidewalk to hermetically seal the interior. Just as there is no front door, there is also no sign or logo identifying the store, simply a twelve-foot-tall (4-meter-tall) aluminum box floating above the sidewalk.

As in his New York epicenter, Koolhaas designed a wooden staircase with multiple functions: Aside from joining the first and second floors, the staircase also provides bleacher-style seating for women waiting to try on shoes and shoppers

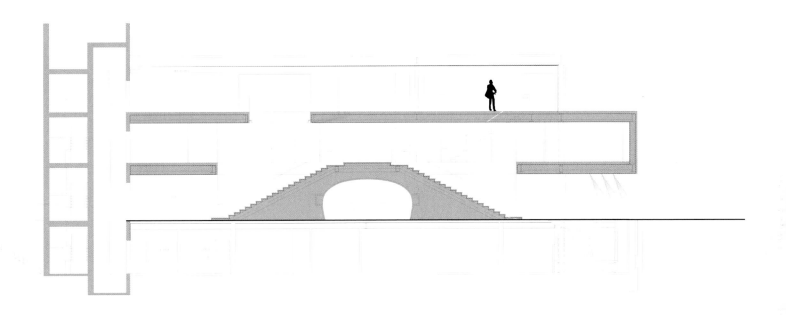

attending the cultural performances Prada promises will take place—though, several years after the opening of the New York store, such events have yet to materialize. Underneath the symmetrical rise of the wood-covered staircase is a vaulted area that's something of a time capsule of Prada's history: The mirrored vault creates distorted fun-house reflections of old-fashioned wood-and-glass display cases and a black-and-white checkerboard floor pattern, both memories of the original Prada store, which opened in Milan's Victor Emmanuel Galleria in 1913 as a family-run luggage purveyor.

The walls of the shop's second floor, devoted to women's fashion, are lined in a porous plastic that resembles coral, developed by Koolhaas and called, simply, Sponge. The brittle-looking walls are painted in the signature pale green that's become a colorful shorthand for Prada and still covers almost every surface in the company's non-"epicenter" locations and its in-store boutiques.

The third floor, which Koolhaas calls the "scenario space," is meant to be a constantly changing milieu with an emphasis on display without traditional racks and hangers, more like a giant display window than a standard sales floor. Presently, clothes are hung in clear acrylic boxes and shoes laid out on long tables reminiscent of airport baggage carousels. As in the New York location, dressing rooms are wrapped in glass that transforms from transparent to opaque with the click of a switch. With the epicenters, Koolhaas and Prada have promised a

Opposite: The shop's subdued elevation on Rodeo Drive in Beverly Hills lacks signage or even doors along the street.
Above: Section.

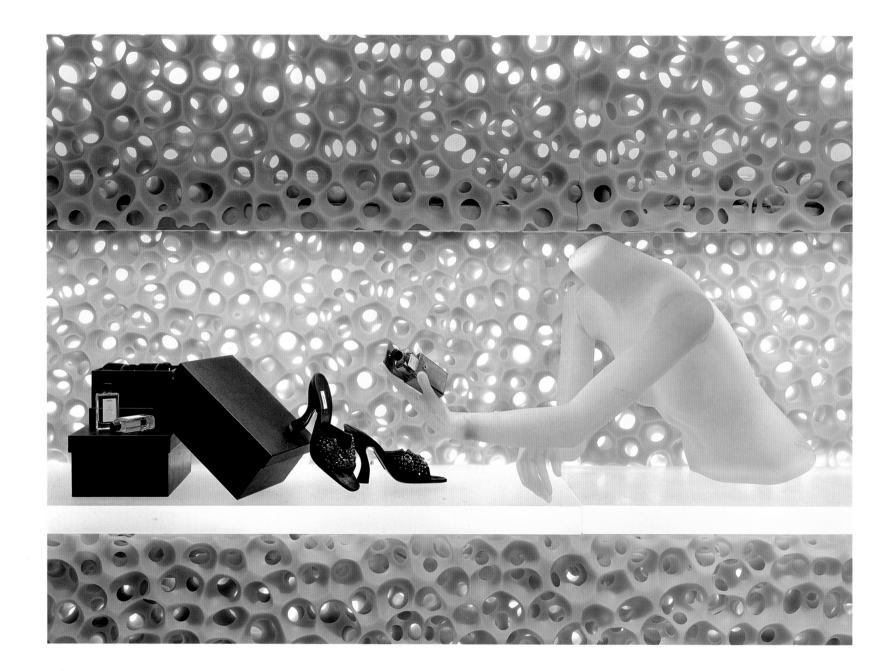

Above: Koolhaas developed Sponge, a porous material resembling coral, which he backlit behind luminous shelves.

Opposite: The walls of Sponge that line the store's second-floor retail area are painted in the signature pale green found throughout Prada's smaller shops and in-store boutiques.

revolutionary reinvention of the act of shopping, but it's difficult to see how revolutionary they really are. If Koolhaas continues to create more Prada epicenters, he will have to compete against the constantly changing and increasingly innovative retail architecture market that he has helped to redefine.

Above: The top floor is crowned with long strips of blue-tinted glass sandwiched between tubular-steel beams.

Opposite, top: A wall of floor-to-ceiling glass overlooks Rodeo Drive.

Opposite, bottom: On the top floor, shoe racks similar to airport baggage carousels extend the same direction as the tubular-steel beams.

Opposite: The main staircase doubles as seating for performances and trying on shoes.
Above: Beneath the staircase, Koolhaas designed display cases and a checkerboard floor pattern based on the original Prada store in Milan, which dates from 1913.

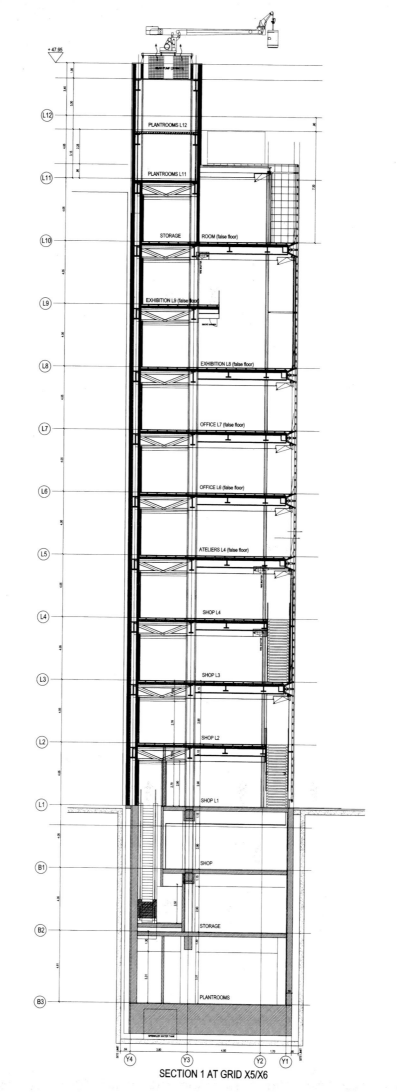

+ 47.95

L12   PLANTROOMS L12

L11   PLANTROOMS L11

L10   STORAGE   ROOM (false floor)

L9   EXHIBITION L9 (false floor)

L8   EXHIBITION L8 (false floor)

L7   OFFICE L7 (false floor)

L6   OFFICE L6 (false floor)

L5   ATELIERS L4 (false floor)

L4   SHOP L4

L3   SHOP L3

L2   SHOP L2

L1   SHOP L1

B1   SHOP

B2   STORAGE

B3   PLANTROOMS

SPRINKLER WATER TANK

Y4   Y3   Y2   Y1

SECTION 1 AT GRID X5/X6

Maison Hermès
Renzo Piano Building Workshop
Tokyo, Japan
2001

BUILDING AREA: 65,325 ft² / 6,071 m²

Tokyo's Ginza, the great commercial district famously plastered with a rainbow of illuminated signs, got a dose of understated European sophistication with the opening of the Renzo Piano–designed Maison Hermès. Piano's design is exquisitely simple: a pair of slender conjoined towers wrapped in a luminous skin of glass blocks. But like the sumptuous products of a luxury brand like Hermès, the building's simplicity belies a sophisticated craft and execution. The sleek cladding is made of more than thirteen thousand custom-fabricated textured glass blocks set into a steel grid. The exterior surfaces of the blocks, developed by Piano and the Vetroarredo glass factory in Florence, were mirror-varnished by hand.

The building consolidates the Parisian label's corporate and retail operations in Tokyo into a single building. Its slender site at the corner of Harumi Dori and Sony Dori in the heart of Ginza is just 39 feet wide by 148 feet long (12 by 45 meters), with a narrow courtyard void rising up the full height of the building. Still, at twelve stories, it projects a strong profile in the Ginza streetscape, in

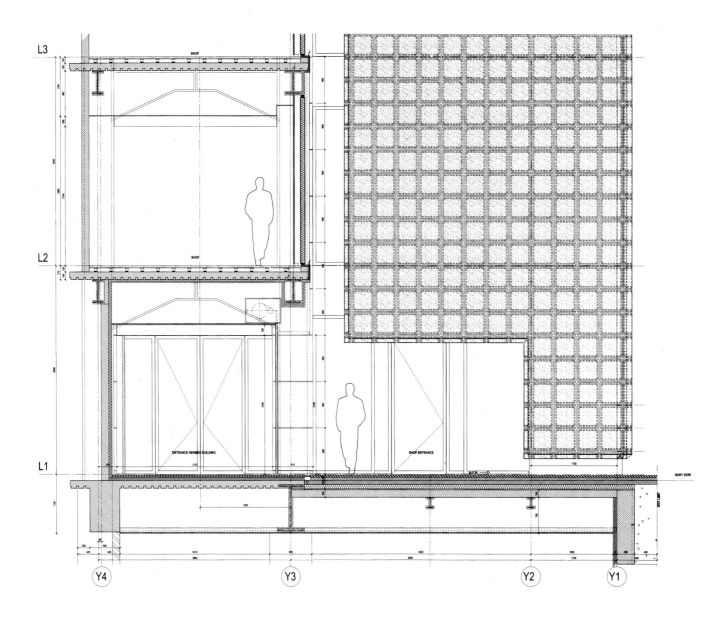

L3

L2

L1

Y4 Y3 Y2 Y1

Above: Section through first and second floors. Opposite: Renzo Piano sheathed the building in an elegant skin of hand-polished glass blocks set into a steel grid. Visible behind the glass facade are staircases connecting shopping levels. Following pages: A narrow shaft between the building's two separate volumes contains separate entrances to the store, offices, art museum, and subway station (left). The glass skin takes on different glowing lines by day and at night, setting the building apart from the garish visual chaos of Tokyo's Ginza district (right).

good measure because of its distinctive glass skin, which is just as striking at night as during the day.

The 65,000-square-foot (6,000-square-meter) building contains five floors of retail, one floor for the design studio, offices on two levels, a mini-museum on the top two floors, and a rooftop garden. The shop, museum, and offices have their own entrances off the narrow courtyard; there is also an entrance to the Tokyo subway station belowground. In typical Piano fashion, his elegant exploration of structure and material resulted in an almost thirty-foot-wide (nine-meter-wide) cantilever that allows for nearly column-free floors all the way to the exterior wall—a blessing for the retailer, especially with such tiny floor plates.

Inside, Piano placed the stairs connecting the first three retail levels against the glass-block exterior so that the movement of shoppers up and down the staircases would animate the facades with activity and differentiate between the shopping floors and the working floors above. Seen from inside the shop, Ginza's bright lights and busy sidewalks create a blur of color and motion behind the textured glass-block walls. The views enliven the shopping experience without distracting too much from the merchandise. The well-appointed interiors, with dark gray carpeting and comfortable club chairs scattered throughout, rely heavily on free-floating racks and elegant vitrines to display Hermès's signature clothes, scarves, ties, and leather goods, as the glass skin wrapping the building on three sides yields only one solid wall per floor.

Above: The sales floors are well-appointed, nearly column-free spaces surrounded by glass-block walls on three sides.

Opposite left: The double-height gallery space recalls the industrial elegance of Pierre Chareau's iconic Maison de Verre in Paris.

Opposite right: An outdoor garden space on the building's top level is surrounded by glass-block walls that blur views of Ginza into a neutral wash.

Following pages: The building presents two very different faces by day and by night, as lights and activity inside create huge but subtle billboards.

On the top two levels, the mini-museum blows open the cozy, intimate feeling of the shopping floors with a lofty, double-height space filled with softly screened daylight. Here, Hermès puts on impeccably mounted art exhibitions by artists such as Hiroshi Sugimoto in a crisp, elegant room reminiscent of the great Maison de Verre in Paris. Like that iconic house, designed by Pierre Chareau in 1927 with walls of glass block set behind exposed steel columns, Maison Hermès combines timeless urban elegance with high-tech innovation. Its architectural expression captures the personality of a storied French brand operating in the frenzied consumer paradise that is Tokyo.

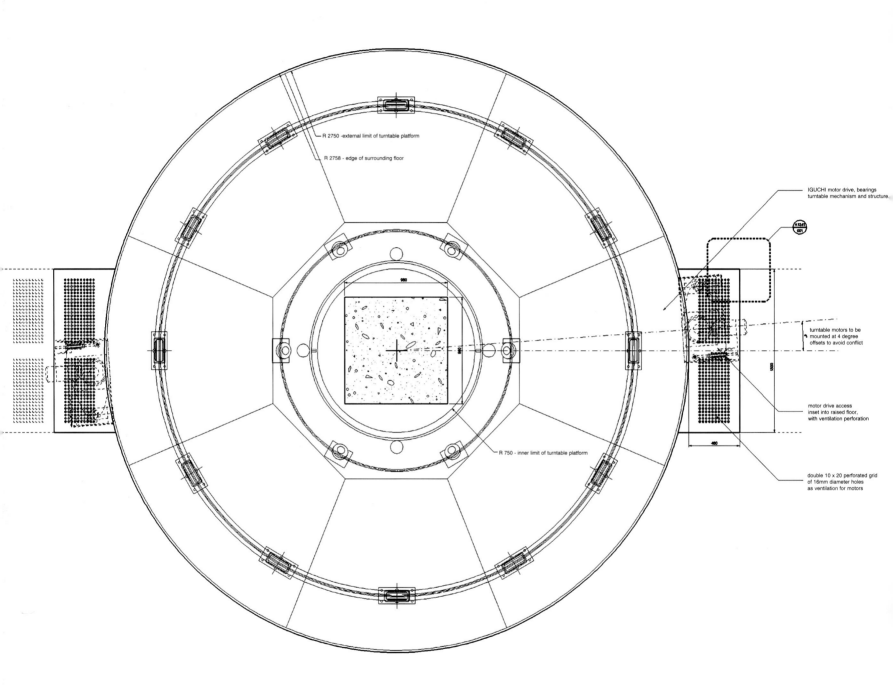

R 2750 -external limit of turntable platform

R 2758 - edge of surrounding floor

IGUCHI motor drive, bearings
turntable mechanism and structure

turntable motors to be
mounted at 4 degree
offsets to avoid conflict

motor drive access
inset into raised floor,
with ventilation perforation

R 750 - inner limit of turntable platform

double 10 x 20 perforated grid
of 16mm diameter holes
as ventilation for motors

Y's Store
Ron Arad Associates
Tokyo, Japan
2003

BUILDING AREA: 570 m² / 6,135 ft²

Yohji Yamamoto belongs to that band of pioneering Japanese fashion designers that includes Issey Miyake, Rei Kawakubo, and Junya Watanabe, a cutting-edge group that put Japan on the fashion-world map. Yamamoto's deconstructed creations combine Asian minimalism with European extravagance à la Vivienne Westwood and a heavy touch of the avant-garde. The Israeli-born, London-based designer and architect Ron Arad is known for aggressive geometric designs that turn convention on its head. Among this maverick designer's more familiar creations is Bookworm, a coiling, free-form bookshelf that seems to defy gravity. So when Yamamoto asked Arad to design a new flagship store for his "Y's" line of clothing in Tokyo, it seemed like the perfect meeting of two rebellious, creative minds.

The 6,135-square-foot (570-square-meter) store occupies a generic space in Tokyo's new Roppongi Hills complex, a shiny city within a city that mixes high-end retail and restaurants with a hotel, office towers, art museum, and TV broadcast studio to create a dense, lively district. Not one to think inside the box,

Arad wanted to overcome the static character of the off-the-shelf volume with a design that was kinetic—literally. He hit on the idea of embedding turntables into the floor so that the displays of Yamamoto's clothes would rotate. Arad installed the turntables around structural columns at the center of the store, which he used as the cores of innovative custom display racks. By day each disk rotates slowly. The motion is nearly imperceptible, but once the store closes for the evening, shopkeepers turn the speed up to create a fun-house display with whirling racks of T-shirts, jeans, and dresses, spinning as if in giant washing machines.

The literal floor rotation is picked up in details throughout the store. On the exterior, Arad installed a skin of glass tube sec-tions extending the full height of the facade. (Of course, the entrance is through a revolving glass door, with the striking Y's logo painted in bright colors on overlapping layers of glass to give the sign depth.) Most striking is the clever display system surrounding the structural columns. Arad wrapped each steel-encased pillar with elliptical aluminum rings, painted a silvery gray, that stack the full height of the column. Each tube can be pulled out and rotated independently of the others to make cas-cading arrangements of hanging racks—Arad compares the stacked rings to coils of a Slinky toy. Similarly, display counters are formed when plastic shelves are clipped into place. The stacking language is continued in the twenty-six-foot-long (eight-meter-long) checkout counter, a gravity-defying arrange-ment of steel slabs painted a bright shade of red. The slabs are

Above: Stacked like the coils of a Slinky, the hanging racks rotate out to create sculptural displays.
Opposite, top: Arad wrapped the store's structural columns with the stacking ring displays. Giant "turntables" concealed in the high-gloss floor spin independently of one another.
Opposite, bottom: Continuing the stacking theme, the checkout counter is made of stacked slabs of epoxy-coated steel.
Following pages: Arad created striking, flexible, and functional displays built of stacked elliptical rings that move individually to create hanging racks or shelves.

cantilevered slightly over one another, generating a visually top-heavy object that could be a piece of minimalist installation art. Some layers are pulled even farther out to create functional built-in shelves.

There's a playful quality to Arad's design, as well as a sense of irreverence for convention—just as in Yamamoto's clothes. The shop uses physical movement rather than an overabundance of design elements to create a lively interior. In fact, there is almost nothing to the store besides the movable tube structures and the lipstick-red counter. But no one could possibly call it a minimalist piece of architecture, and no one would dare call it just another interior.

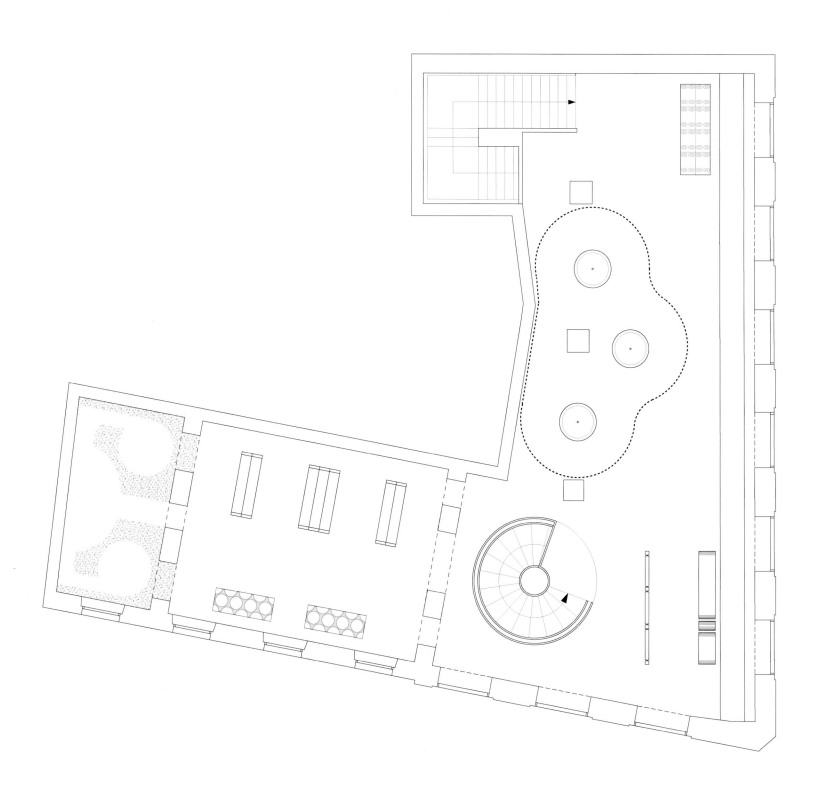

Mandarina Duck Embassy
NL Architects / Droog Design
Paris, France
2001

BUILDING AREA: 3,444 ft² / 320 m²

When it branched out into accessories and clothing to complement its playful, offbeat luggage, the Italian brand Mandarina Duck rethought the look of its retail stores. The company hired the influential Dutch think-tank-cum-design-studio Droog Design to shape its flagship boutique on the tony Rue Saint-Honoré in Paris, which would become a prototype for future outposts. (Mandarina Duck called the Paris store and another flagship in London, by Dutch designer Marcel Wanders, "embassies" while smaller shops in other European cities are referred to as "consulates.") Droog in turn hired the young Amsterdam-based practice NL Architects to three-dimensionally develop design ideas, with Droog principals Renny Ramakers and Gijs Bakker acting as curators and art directors for the concepts generated by NL Architects' four partners.

NL developed what it calls, not entirely without irony, a "store without architecture." Indeed, the floors, walls, and ceilings in the two-level, 3,440-square-foot (320-square-meter) space are all painted white and the only design elements are a series of playful, surrealist display units the architects refer to as cocoons. As

Previous pages: NL Architects and Droog Design created a variety of playful, innovative display systems, including a wall of colorful elastic straps that hold bags in place (bottom, center) and the "incubator," a science fiction-worthy fixture where shoppers grab objects secured in a glass vitrine with built-in gloves (top left).

Above: The "Inverse Clothes Rack" is a steel-clad pod that rolls open to reveal built-in shelving.

Opposite: The aluminum 'Pinwall' features metal rods that slide back to create a void in which handbags, clutches, and other irregularly shaped products can be displayed.

they point out, "space can be considered the biggest luxury of all." Theory aside, this strategy of animating a completely neutral shell with quirky, colorful displays is a practical one: Instead of architecture, Mandarina Duck could give its stores a visual identity with a completely changeable collection of cleverly designed fixtures that could fit out any one of their stores. The design values are strong but also easily and relatively inexpensively swapped out to freshen the label's image, an important consideration in the fickle world of retail.

Mandarina Duck has always valued strong colors, as seen in its bright yellow duck logo and the bold splashes of red, yellow, and orange on its bags, watches, sunglasses, and sportswear. Droog and NL translated that sensibility in the thoroughly origi-

nal display units that fill the shop with splashes of color and texture. The most subdued are the "Pinwall," an aluminum wall that holds purses and portfolios in the voids created by pushing back a grid of metal rods and the "Inverse Clothes Rack," a circular steel pod that conceals racks and shelves along its interior. From there, the sky is the limit. The "Palette Tunnel" features translucent plastic shelves cast from industrial palettes and lit from below to create a glowing mini-room. On the "Rubber Wall," merchandise is held effortlessly in place by thick elastic bands in bold yellow, green, and red. And the circular dressing rooms are surrounded by stalks of hundreds of fiberglass rods anchored to a metal base. The architects liken the dressing areas surrounded by strange, bendable "curtains" to clearings in a cornfield.

Above and opposite: The only concrete piece of "architecture" in the store is a rotating staircase in Mandarina Duck yellow that theoretically drops shoppers off at a new destination every time they climb the stairs.

Following pages: The architects hid the dressing rooms behind stalks of fiberglass rods (left) and used bendable "curtains" to define space within the store (right).

There is one piece of actual architecture, but even that refuses to stay put—literally. A curving helix-shaped spiral stair, which is painted in the label's signature rubber-duck yellow, rotates slowly in place like a giant rotisserie. The architects compare shoppers' experience of spinning while moving up or down to being "beamed up," Star Trek fashion. They cite one practical advantage to the rotating stairs: Every time shoppers climb it, they (theoretically) arrive in a different spot. Every visit therefore feels different, even if nothing inside the store has changed. For all their quirky playfulness, Droog and NL Architects' fun-house of fixtures are functional, changeable, and highly memorable— an accomplishment that is not without irony considering the Paris store closed in February 2003, only twenty-eight months after it first opened.

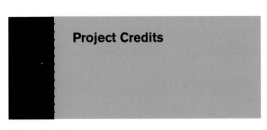

Project Credits

Introduction

Prada New York Epicenter

Location New York, New York, USA
Year 2001
Building Area 23,575 ft2 / 2190 m2
Client Prada
Architect Office for Metropolitan Architecture (OMA)
Principals Rem Koolhaas and Ole Scheeren
Project Architects Timothy Archambault, Eric Chang
Associated Architect Architecture Research Office (ARO)
Engineers Arup (structural), Leslie E. Robertson
Associates (strucural)
Lighting Kugler Tillotson Associates
Curtains Inside-Outside
Wall Paper 2x4
Movable Furniture Seufert

BEST Products Indeterminate Facade Showroom

Location Houston, Texas, USA
Year 1974
Building Area 65,280 ft2 / 6,065 m2
Client BEST Products Company
Architect SITE
Principal James Wines
Architect of Record Maple-Jones Associates

BEST Products Catalog Showroom

Location Langhorne, Pennsylvania, USA
Year 1978
Building Area 32,000 ft2 / 2,973 m2
Client BEST Products Company
Architect Venturi, Scott Brown and Associates
Principals Robert Venturi and Denise Scott Brown

Basco Showroom

Location Philadelphia, Pennsylvania, USA
Year 1976
Building Area 80,000 ft2 / 7,432 m2
Client Basco. Inc.
Architect Venturi, Scott Brown and Associates
Principals Robert Venturi and Denise Scott Brown

Calvin Klein Flagship

Location New York, New York, USA
Year 1996
Building Area 10,000 ft2 / 929 m2
Client Calvin Klein
Architect John Pawson

Dior Omotesando

Location Tokyo, Japan
Year 2004
Building Area 16,060 ft2 / 1,492 m2
Client Christian Dior

Architects SANAA (exterior), Christian Dior Couture
Architecture Department, Architecture & Associés, Higo &
Associates (interior)
Principals Kazuyo Sejima and Ryue Nishizawa (SANAA);
Hedi Slimane (Christian Dior Couture); Pierre Beucler and
Jean-Christophe Poggioli (Architecture & Associés); Isao
Higo (Higo & Associates)
Engineers Sasaki Mutsuro Structural Consultants (struc-
tural), P.T. Morimura & Associates (mechanical)
General Contractor Shimizu Corporation

Federation Square

Location Melbourne, Australia
Year 2004
Building Area 473,600 ft2 / 44,000 m2
Client Federation Square Management
Architects Lab architecture studio in association with
Bates Smart
Principals Donald Bates, Peter Davidson
Engineers atelier one (structural), Hyder Consulting (struc-
tural), Bonacci Group (structural), Connell Wagner (civil),
Hyder Consulting (civil), AHW Consulting Engineers
(services), Arup (fire)
Lighting Lighting Design Partnership
Signage and Graphic Design tomato / gary emery design
General Contractor Multiplex

Publix by the Bay

Location Miami Beach, Florida, USA
Year 1999
Building Area 150,000 ft2 / 13,900 m2
Client Publix
Architect Wood + Zapata, Inc.
Principals Benjamin Wood, Carlos Zapata
Project Team Wyatt Porter Brown, Victoria Steven, Fred
Botelho, Eric Klingler, Rolando Mendoza, Anthony
Montalto, Pamela Torres
Engineers Leslie E. Robertson Associates (structural),
Thomas Engineering (MEP), Bermello, Ajamil & Partners
(civil)
General Contractor Keene Construction

Apple SoHo

Location New York, New York, USA
Year 2001
Building Area 16,000 ft2 / 1,486 m2
Client Apple Computer, Inc.
Architect Bohlin Cywinski Jackson
Principals Peter Q. Bohlin, Jon C. Jackson, Karl Backus
Project Team Karl Backus, Rosa Sheng, Ben McDonald,
Colleen Caulliez, Michael Waltner
Associated Architect Ronnette Riley Architects
Design Associate and Fixture Design Eight Inc.
Engineers Dewhurst Macfarlane & Partners (structural),
Flack and Kurtz (MEP)
Lighting ISP Design
General Contractor JT Magen & Company

Qiora Store and Spa

Location New York, New York, USA
Year 2000
Building Area 1,500 ft2 / 140m2
Client Shiseido Cosmetics
Architect Architecture Research Office (ARO)
Principals Stephen Cassell, Adam Yarinsky
Project Manager Scott Abrams
Project Team Josh Pulver, Eunice Seng, Rossalune Shieh,
Kim Yao

Selected Projects

Prada Aoyama Epicenter

Location Tokyo, Japan
Year 2003
Building Area 30,785 ft2 / 2,860 m2
Client Prada Japan Co., Ltd.
Architect Herzog & de Mueron
Principals Jacques Herzog, Pierre de Mueron
Project Manager Takenaka Corporation
Project Team Michio Jinushi, Kenji Takeshima, Shinobu
Chiba, Shuji Ishikawa, Ken Kurita
General Contractor Tanenaka Corporation

MPreis Wenns Supermarket

Location Wenns, Austria
Year 2001
Building Area 12,056 ft2 / 1120 m2
Client MPreis GmbH
Architect Köberl
Principals Rainer Köberl, Astrid Tschapeller
Project Manager Klaus Schmücking
Engineer Alfred Brunnsteiner (structural)
General Contractors Thurnen Bau, Schlosserei Starck,
Laas Leichtdach

Issey Miyake Tribeca

Location New York, New York, USA
Year 2001
Building Area 14,664 ft2 / 1,362 m2
Client Issey Miyake USA Corp.
Architects G Tects, LLC, Frank Gehry and Associates
Principals Gordon Kipping, Frank Gehry
Project Manager Lissa Parrott
Project Team Bryan Bullen, Monica Tiulescu, Yu Duk So,
Shirley Ting
Mural Artist Alejandro Gehry
Engineers Gilsanz Murray Steficek (structural), Mariano
Gerazounis & Jaffe Associates (mechanical)
Lighting L'observatoire International Lighting Designers &
Consultants
Preservation Consultant Intergrated Conservation
Resources
Landmarks Consultant Higgins & Quasebarth
Sculpture Fabricator A. Zahner Company, Architectural
Metal, Paul Martin
Fixture and Furnishings Fabricator Atlas Industries
General Contractor Shimizu Corporation

Asprey New York Flagship

Location New York, New York, USA
Year 2003
Building Area 30,000 ft2 / 2,787 m2
Client Asprey & Garrard
Architect Foster and Partners
Principal Norman Foster
Project Team Graham Phillips, Marco Gamini, Bernd
Truempler, Armstrong Yakubu, Giles Robinson, Kevin
Carrucan, Guy Herschell, Gloria Tsi, Michael Ng, Kathleen
Feagin, Matthew Abbott
Interior Furnishings Mlinaric, Henry, and Zervidachi
Architect of Record Leclere Associates
Project Manager Gardner and Theobald
Engineers Cantor Seinuk Group (structural), Thomas J
Fiskaa Engineering (MEP)
Lighting Kondos Roberts

Asprey London Flagship

Location London, England, UK
Year 2004
Building Area 50,000 ft2 / 4,645 m2
Client Asprey & Garrard
Architect Foster and Partners
Principal Norman Foster
Project Team Graham Phillips, Giles Robinson, Filo Russo,
Andries Kruger, Winky Wong, Raza Zahid, Gloria Tsai,
Ryan Von Ruben, Michael Ng, Abel Maciel
Engineers Alan Baxter Associates (structural), Troup
Bywaters & Anders (MEP)
Interior Design David Milarnic
Lighting Kondos Roberts

De Brink Center

Location Hengelo, The Netherlands
Year 1999
Building Area 676,700 ft2 / 35,000 m2
Client ING Vastgoed, Den Hague
Architect Bolles + Wilson
Principals Peter Wilson and Prof. Julia Bolles-Wilson
Project Assistant Axel Kempers
Associated Architect Bureau Bouwkunde, Rotterdam

Selfridges

Location Birmingham, England, UK
Year 2003
Building Area 269,000 ft2 / 25,000 m2
Client Selfridges & Co.
Architect Future Systems
Principals Jan Kaplicky, Amanda Levete
Project Manager Faithful + Gould
Engineer Arup (structure, services, facade)
General Contractor Laing O'Rourke
Subcontractors Sir Robert McAlpine (main frame), Haden
Young (MEP), Haran Glass (glazing), 5M (envelope),
James + Taylor (disc manufacturer), Baris/Jordan (steel
panelling), Shotcrete (sprayed concrete), Diespeker
(GRP/GRG)

Louis Vuitton Omotesando

Location Tokyo, Japan
Year 2002
Building Area 35,080 ft2 / 3,259 m2
Client Louis Vuitton Japan
Architects Jun Aoki & Associates (exterior), Louis Vuitton
Architecture Department (interior)
Principals Jun Aoki (Jun Aoki & Associates), Eric Carlson,
David McNulty (Louis Vuitton Architecture Department)
Project Managers Shinya Kamuro, Norihito Maezaki,
Hiroaki Namba, Marie-Eve Bidard, Laetitia Perrin
Associated Architect Higo Design Associates
Furniture Design Studio Power
Lighting George Sexton Associates
Interior Contractor Takashimaya Space Create
General Contractor Shimizu Corporation

Louis Vuitton Roppongi Hills

Location Tokyo, Japan
Year 2003
Building Area 12,345 ft2 / 1,147 m2
Client Louis Vuitton Japan
Architects Jun Aoki & Associates, Studio Aurelio Clementi,
Louis Vuitton Architecture Department
Principals Jun Aoki (Jun Aoki & Associates), Aurelio
Clementi (Studio Aurelio Clementi), Eric Carlson (Louis

Vuitton Architecture Department)
Project Managers Ryuji Nakamura, Marie-Eve Bidard
Project Team Noriko Nagayama, Irene Antolini, Gettina
Schepis, Laetitia Perrin, Mathurin Hardel
Associated Architect Higo Design Associates
Lighting George Sexton Associates
Graphic Design FLAME, Inc.
Floor Imaging Design SUN Produce, Speaking Pictures
Fabric Design NUNO
Lighting Fabrication Yamagiwa Inc.
Interior Contractor Takashimaya Space Create
General Contractor and Engineer Shimizu Corporation

Louis Vuitton Ginza Namiki

Location Tokyo, Japan
Year 2004
Building Area 22,970 ft2 / 21,334 m2
Client Louis Vuitton Japan
Architects Jun Aoki & Associates, Louis Vuitton
Architecture Department
Principal Jun Aoki
Project Managers Takayoshi Nagaishi, Eiri Ota
Project Team Masako Asai, Tsunetaka Ueda, Katsuyki
Iwakiri
Associated Architects Higo & Associates
Lighting George Sexton Associates
General Contractor Shimizu Corporation

Louis Vuitton New York

Location New York, New York, USA
Year 2004
Building Area 88,930 ft2 / 8,262 m2
Client Louis Vuitton North America
Architects Jun Aoki & Associates (exterior), Peter Marino
Associates (interior)
Principals Jun Aoki (Jun Aoki & Associates), Peter Marino
(Peter Marino Associates)
Project Managers Takayoshi Nagaishi, Maria Wilthew, Paul
Garret
Associated Architects Louis Vuitton Architecture
Department, The Phillips Group
Lighting George Sexton Associates
Engineers Severud Associates (strucural), Lazlo Bodak
Engineers (MEP)
Facade Consultant RA Heintges
Facade Contractor Josef Gartner & Co.
General Contractor Shawmut Design and Construction

Forum Flagship

Location São Paulo, Brazil
Year 2000
Building Area 12,205 ft2 / 1,144 m2
Client Forum
Architect Isay Weinfeld
Project Manager Monica Cappa Santoni
Collaborator Domingos Pascali
Project Team Ana Luisa Cunha Pinheiro, Fabio Rudnik,
Flavia Oide
General Contractor Fairbanks & Pilnik

Clube Chocolate

Location São Paulo, Brazil
Year 2003
Building Area 18,665 ft2 / 1,734 m2
Client Clube Chocolate
Architect Isay Weinfeld
Project Manager Elena Scarabotolo
Collaborator Domingos Pascali

Project Team Carolina Maluhy, Flavia Oide, Juliana Scalizi
Landscape Design Isabel Duprat Paisagismo
General Contractor Fairbanks & Pilnik

Undercover Lab

Location Tokyo, Japan
Year 2001
Building Area 6,878 ft2 / 639 m2
Client Under Cover Co., Ltd.
Architect Klein Dytham architecture
Principals Astrid Klein, Mark Dytham
Project Manager Taku Iwata
Project Team Astrid Klein, Mark Dytham, Yukinari
Hisayama, Yuko Iwamatsu
Engineers Structured Environment (structural), ES
Associates (mechanical)
General Contractor Aoki Corporation

Novy Smíchov Shopping Center

Location Prague, Czech Republic
Year 2001
Building Area 1,865,000 ft2 / 173,250 m2
Architect D3A Fiala, Prouza, Zima
Client Carrefour
Principals Tomás Prouza, Jaroslav Zima
Project Mangers Tomás Prouza, Jaroslav Zima, Sabina
Mestanova, Prof. Martin Rajnis
Project Team Tomás Prouza, Jaroslav Zima, Sabina
Mestanova, Prof. Martin Rajni, Milan Bulva, Hynek Holisˇ,
Alena Jandová, David Jarosˇ, Ondrˇej Kafka, Martin Kloda,
David Lédl, Tomásˇ Pechman, Jan Prˇikryl, Lucie Sˇtorková
General Contractor Skanska

l.a. Eyeworks

Location Los Angeles, California, USA
Year 2002
Building Area 1,150 ft2 / 107 m2
Clients Gai Gherardi and Barbara McReynolds
Architect Neil M. Denari Architects, Inc.
Principal Neil Denari
Project Architect Duks Koschitz
Engineer Gordon Polon (structural)
Mobile Furniture Fabrication K.B. Manufacturing
Lighting L.D.A.
Project Superintendent Peter Jones
Graphic Design Carmen Hammerer
General Contractor Duran and Associates

MPreis Wattens Supermarket

Location Wattens, Austria
Year 2003
Building Area 57,015 ft2 / 5,297 m2
Client MPreis GmbH
Architects Dominique Perrault Architecte
Principal Dominique Perrault
Project Managers Claudia Dieling, Ralf Levedag
Project Team Anne Speicher, Andreas Aschmann
Associated Architect RPM Architects

Carlos Miele Flagship

Location New York, New York, USA
Year 2003
Building Area 3,230 ft2 / 500 m2
Client Carlos Miele
Architect Asymptote
Principals Hani Rashid, Lise-Anne Couture

Project Architect Jill Leckner
Project Team Noboru Ota, John Cleater, Peter Horner, Cathy Jones
Project Assistants Micheal Levy Bajar, Janghwan Cheon, Teresa Cheung, Mary Ellen Cooper, Shinichiro Himematsu, Michael Huang, Lamia Jallad, Ana Sa, Markus Schnierle, Yasmin Shahamiri
Engineers Kam Chiu, Andre Tomas Chaszar
Lighting Focus Lighting
Fabricator 555 International
Contractor Vanguard Construction & Development

Fünf Höfe (Five Courtyards)

Location Munich, Germany
Year 2003
Building Area 839,585 ft2 / 78,000 m2
Client Fünf Höfe GmbH
Architect Herzog & de Mueron
Principals Jacques Herzog, Pierre de Mueron
Project Team Sascha Arnold, Konstanze Beelitz, Andrea Bernhard, Rolf Berninger, Silvia Beyer, Jean-Claude Cadalbert, Enrica Ferrucci, Agnes Förster, Eric Frisch, Martin Fröhlich, Jacques Herzog, Robert Hösl, Tim Hupe, Susanne Kleinlein, Susanna Knopp, Milena Kondoferska, Katharina Kovarbasic, Martin Krapp, Jan Kurz, Julia Lingenfelder, Pierre de Meuron, Ursula Müller, Fabian Ochs, Matthias Pektor, Jan Frederik Peters, Heiner Reimers, Peter Reinhardt, Daniel Reisch, Christoph Röttinger, Florian Schmidhuber, Christian Schühle, Korinna Thielen, Markus Wassmer

Vitra

Location New York, New York, USA
Year 2002
Building Area 13,000 ft2 / 1,208 m2
Client Vitra USA
Architect ROY
Principal Lindy Roy
Project Team Lindy Roy, Sandra Donough, Tracy Geraldez, Jason Lee, Barbara Ludescher, Gernot Riether, Heidi Werner, Mark Kroeckel (Openshop|Studio)
Architect of Record Peter Himmelstein Architect
Engineers Anchor Consulting (strucural), Stanislav Slutsky (mechanical)
Graphic Design 2x4
General Contractor Vanguard Construction and Development

Migros Shopping Center and School

Location Lucerne, Switzerland
Year 2000
Building Area 313,770 ft2 / 29,150 m2
Clients Genossenschaft Migros, Hotel Schweizerhof
Architect Diener & Diener Architekten
Principal Roger Diener
Site Engineer TGS Partner Architekten
Landscape Architect Stefan Koepfli
General Contractor Bucher + Diller

Prada Los Angeles Epicenter

Location Los Angeles, California, USA
Year 2004
Building Area 24,000 ft2 / 2,230 m2
Client Prada USA
Architect Office for Metropolitan Architecture (OMA)/AMO
Principals Rem Koolhaas, Ole Scheeren
Project Managers Eric Chang, Jessica Rothschild,

Amale Andraos
Project Team Christian Bandi, Catarina Canas, David Moore, Mark Watanabe, Torsten Schroeder, Jocelyn Low, Keren Engelman, Ali Kops, Jeffrey Johnson
AMO Technology Markus Schaefer, Clemens Weisshaar, Reed Kram
AMO Content Nicolas Firket, Michael Rock, Joakim Dahlqvist, Reed Kram, Stephen Wang, Richard Wang, Sung Kim, Dan Michaelson, Leigh Devine
Executive Architect Brand+Allen Architects
Engineer Arup (structure, services)
Lighting Kugler Tillotson Associates
Facade and Skylight Dewhurst McFarlane
Lift Wall Hamilton Engineering
Curtain Inside-Outside
Wallpaper and Graphic Design 2x4
General Contractor Plant Construction

Maison Hermés

Location Tokyo, Japan
Year 2001
Building Area 65,325 ft2 / 6,071 m2
Client Hermés Japan
Architect Renzo Piano Building Workshop
Principal Renzo Piano
Project Manager P. Vincent
Project Team L. Couton, G. Ducci, P. Hendier, S. Ishida, F. La Rivière, C. Kuntz; C. Colson, Y. Kyrkos
Associated Architect Architecture Intérieure (Rena Dumas)
Consulting Executive Architect Takenaka Corporation Design Department
Engineer Arup (structure, services)
Landscape Architect K. Tanaka
Sculpture S. Shingu

Y's Store

Location Tokyo, Japan
Year 2003
Building Area 6,135 ft2 / 570 m2
Client Yohji Yamamoto, Inc.
Architect Ron Arad Associates
Principal Ron Arad
Project Architects Asa Bruno
Project Team James Foster, Paul Gibbons
Executive Architect Studio Mebius (Shiro Nakada, Satoru Ishihara)
Lighting iGuzzini
Loop Contractor Marzorati-Ronchetti
Floor Contractor ABC Flooring
General Contractors Build Co., Minoru Kawamura

Mandarina Duck Embassy

Location Paris, France
Year 2000
Year Dismantled 2003
Building Area 3,444 ft2 / 320 m2
Client Mandarina Duck
Architects NL Architects, Droog Design
Principals Pieter Bannenberg, Bernd Druffel, Kirtsen Huesig, Afaina de Jong, Rolf Touzimsky (NL Architects), Renny Ramakers, Gijs Bakker (Droog Design)
Project Team Caro Baumann, Bernd Druffel, Kirsten Huesig, Afaina de Jong, Rolf Touzimsky, Stijn Roodnat

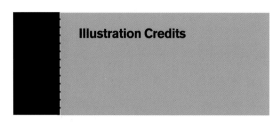

Illustration Credits

Further Reading

Soren Aagaard, courtesy Future Systems: 62, 66–69
©Daichi Ano: 75, 76
Daichi Ano, courtesy Louis Vuitton, France: 78–82, 84–85
©Richard Barnes 145b, 146, 148
©Benny Chan: 116–118
Peter Clarke, courtesy Lab architecture studio: 12l, 12c
©Jimmy Cohrssen: 11, 74, 77, 83, 85r, 86–91, 186t, 186bc, 187t, 188–190, 192–193
Löic Couhon, courtesy Renzo Piano Building Workshop: 171bl
©Richard Davies: 63, 64, 70, 71
Michel Denancé, courtesy Renzo Piano Building Workshop: 169–170, 171 (except bl), 172–175
©Todd Eberle: 10r
©Floto+Warner: 158, 160–165
©Dennis Gilbert/VIEW: 50–51
©Jeff Goldberg/ESTO, courtesy Wood+Zapata Architects: 13
©Roland Halbe: 152–155
Andrew Hobbs, courtesy Lab architecture studio: 12r
©David Joseph: 15
©Ralph Kämena: 186br, 187bc, 187br, 191
Eric Lagniel, courtesy ROY: 144, 145t, 147, 149
©Armin Linke: 7–8
©Johannes Marburg: 46–49
André Morin, courtesy Dominique Perrault Architecte: 122–124, 126–127
Nacasa + Partners, courtesy Herzog & de Mueron: 18–19, 21–23, 25–27
Nacasa + Partners, courtesy Y's Yohji Yamamoto: 178–183
Courtesy NL Architects: 186bl, 186–187b, 187 bl
Álvaro Povoa, courtesy Isay Weinfeld: 98–101
Tuca Reinés, courtesy Isay Weinfeld: 94–97
©Christian Richters: 20, 24l, 56–59
©Lukas Schaller: 30–35
Courtesy SITE: 9l
©Filip Slapal: 110–113
©Margherita Spiluttini: 138–141
©Kozo Takayama: 104–107
Courtesy Venturi, Scott Brown and Associates: 9r, 10l, 10c
©Paul Warchol: 14, 38–43, 130–132, 134–135
Nigel Young, courtesy Foster and Partners: 52–53

Buchanan, Peter. *Renzo Piano Building Workshop: Complete Works, Vols. 1-4*. London: Phaidon, 1999–2003.

Castle, Helen and Martin Pawley. *Fashion & Architecture*. New York: Academy, 2001.

Chung, Chuihua Judy, et al., eds. *The Harvard Design School Guide to Shopping*. Köln: Taschen, 2002

Collings, Matthew. *Matthew Collings Talks to Ron Arad*. London: Phaidon, 2004.

Couture, Lise Anne and Hani Rashid. *Asymptote: Flux*. London: Phaidon, 2002.

Denari, Neil M. *Gyroscopic Horizons*. New York: Princeton Architectural Press, 1999.

Droog Design. *Simply Droog*. Amsterdam: Droog, 2004.

Field, Marcus. *Future Systems*. London: Phaidon, 1999.

Frame. *Klein Dytham: Frame Monographs of Contemporary Interior Architects*. Basel: Birkhauser, 2001.

Hata, Kyoriji. *Louis Vuitton Japan: The Building of Luxury*. New York: Assouline, 2004.

Herzog, Jacques et al. *Prada Aoyama Tokyo*. Milan: Fondazione Prada, 2004.

Herzog, Jacques et al. *Herzog & de Meuron: Natural History*. Baden: Lars Müller, 2003.

Institute of Store Planners Staff. *Stores and Retail Spaces 5*. New York: Watson-Guptill, 2004.

Jenkins, David. *Norman Foster Works 1–4*. New York: Prestel, 2003–2004.

Kaplicky, Jan. *Confessions: Principles Architecture Process Life*. New York: Academy, 2002.

Koolhaas, Rem et al. *Projects for Prada Part 1*. Milan: Fondazione Prada, 2001.

Lefteri, Chris and Ron Arad. *Metals: Materials for Inspirational Design*. East Sussex: Rotovision, 2004.

Miyake, Issey et al. *Issey Miyake: Making Things*. Zurich: Scalo, 1999.

Pawley, Martin. *Norman Foster: A Global Architecture*. New York: Universe,1999.

Pawson, John. *John Pawson: Themes and Projects*. London: Phaidon, 2002.

Pegler, Martin M. *Stores of the Year*. New York: Visual Reference, 2001.

Perrault, Dominique. *With Dominique Perrault Architect*. Basel: Birkhauser, 1999.

Piano, Renzo. *On Tour with Renzo Piano*. London: Phaidon, 2004.

Ramakers, Renny and Gijs Bakker. *Droog Design*. Amsterdam: Boom, 1998.

Richters, Christian. *Bolles + Wilson: Recent Buildings and Projects*. Basel: Birkhauser, 1997.

Riewoldt, Otto, ed. *Brandscaping: Worlds of Experience in Retail Design*. Basel: Birkhauser, 2002.

Rosa, Joseph et al. *Roy: Design Series 1*. Corte Madera: Ginkgo, 2003.

Staedler, Laurent. *Dominique Perrault*. Milan: Electa Architecture, 2002.

Sudjic, Deyan. *John Pawson Works*. London: Phaidon, 2000.

Van Tilburg, Carolien. *PowerShop: New Japanese Retail Design*. Basel: Birkhauser, 2002.

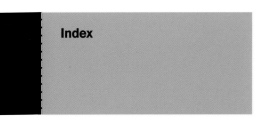

Index

Phaidon Press Limited
Regent's Wharf
All Saints Street
London N1 9PA

Phaidon Press Inc.
180 Varick Street
New York, NY 10014

www.phaidon.com

First published 2005
Reprinted in paperback 2008
© 2005 Phaidon Press Limited

ISBN 978 0 7148 4862 4

A CIP catalogue record for this book is available from the British Library.

Printed in Hong Kong